THE CAN

Other titles of interest

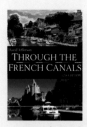

Through the French Canals 12th edition
David Jefferson
ISBN 9781 4081 0381 4

This is a guide to the French canals and rivers of France for those who wish to enjoy the wonderful scenery of rural France by exploring the waterways. It is helpful too for those who are on passage from the English Channel to the Mediterranean. The book is packed with colour photographs and practical information on local facilities, distances, depths, bridge heights, tunnel lengths and masses of useful tips on negotiating locks, plus invaluable translations of useful French terms which will help you on your cruise.

The Adlard Coles Book of EuroRegs for Inland Waterways 3rd edition
Marian Martin
ISBN 9781 4081 0141 4

The CEVNI rules are set out in an easy-to-follow format covering waterway signs, signals, flags and lights, markings on vessels, procedures in tunnels, locks and weirs, overtaking rules, berthing, and buoyage and landmarks are also explained. It also forms the basis of the RYA test for the International Certificate of Competence.

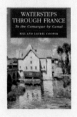

*Watersteps through France
– to the Camargue by Canal*
Bill and Laurel Cooper
ISBN 9780 7136 4391 6

When Bill and Laurel Cooper decided to spend the winter in the south of France, they took their Dutch barge *Hosanna* there by following a route through the canals and rivers of France. This book describes their journey, the people they met and some of the local folklore and customs they experienced.

THE CANAL DU MIDI

A CRUISER'S GUIDE

BERND WILFRED KIESSLER

ADLARD COLES NAUTICAL
LONDON

Maps

The maps serve only for guidance and are not for navigation; they do not replace in any way the official charts for the area. The author wishes to express his gratitude to Monika Fritsch und Thomas Schmidt, Maison de la France in Frankfurt am Main, and also Friederike Haussmann, Le Boat in Bad Vilbel, for advice and help. Bibliographic Information was provided by the German National Library.

Published by Adlard Coles Nautical
an imprint of Bloomsbury Publishing Plc
50 Bedford Square, London WC1B 3DP
www.adlardcoles.com

Copyright © 1990 and 2008 Edition Maritim GmbH

Copyright © English language text Adlard Coles Nautical 2009

First UK edition 2009

Reprinted 2012, 2013, 2014, 2016, 2017

Published in 2008 by Edition Maritim GmbH, Raboisen 8, D-20095 Hamburg with the title *Canal du Midi*

ISBN 978-1-4081-1273-1

A CIP catalogue record for this book is available from the British Library.

This book is produced using paper that is made from wood grown in managed, sustainable forests. It is natural, renewable and recyclable.
The logging and manufacturing processes conform to the environmental regulations of the country of origin.

Printed and bound in India by Replika Press Pvt. Ltd.

Note: while all reasonable care has been taken in the publication of this edition, the publisher takes no responsibility for the use of the methods or products described in the book.

CONTENTS

INTRODUCTION

There are many good reasons for navigating the Canal du Midi and other southern French waterways, not least for their fascinating history.

The Canal du Midi is over 300 years old and is one of the oldest sections of the extensive network of navigable French waterways. Much of the architecture, including the characteristic oval locks, dates back to the origins of the canal. Those keen on canal history will discover much of interest, often in the most unexpected places.

Because the Canal du Midi has been officially declared a World Heritage site by Unesco, its future existence, which at one time was under threat, now seems finally assured. What is more, the work to preserve it is being carried out with the necessary sensitivity that such a great engineering feat merits.

There is also a practical reason for navigating these waterways. Boat owners can avoid passage-making around Spain and into the Mediterranean (or in the opposite direction) if their boats are less than 30 metres in length,

The lock keeper's companion watches with interest as boats go by.

with a beam less than 5.20 metres, a height above waterline less than 3.30 metres and a draught not exceeding 1.40 metres. From the Atlantic, they can then sail into the broad estuary of the Gironde towards Bordeaux and leave the inland waterways again at the following places:

- Port-la-Nouvelle via the Canal de la Robine

- South of Agde via the mouth of the River Hérault, leaving the Canal du Midi at the legendary round lock

- Through the canals of the town of Sète

- Le Grau-du-Roi via the Canal Maritime and Aigues-Mortes, accessed from the Canal du Rhône à Sète

- Via the Petit Rhône to its mouth at Stes Maries-de-la-Mer (restricted draught only)

- Finally via the Rhône itself from Arles down to the sea at Port-Saint-Louis

These exits to the Mediterranean are of course also available to all those coming down the Rhône who want to travel as far west as possible on sheltered inland waters before venturing out to sea.

Typical scene on the Canal du Midi with a traditional stone bridge.

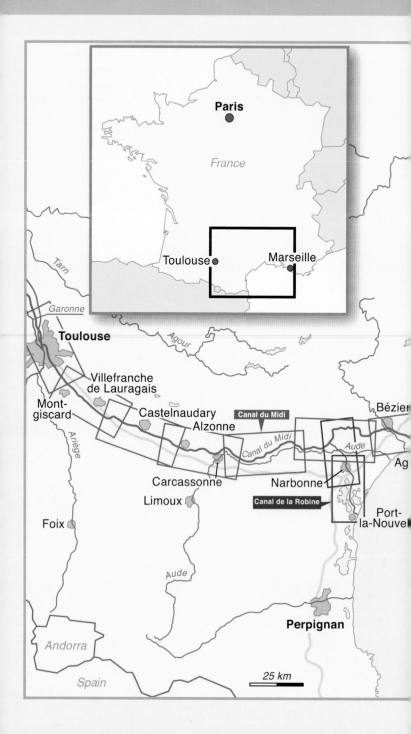

Paris

France

Toulouse

Marseille

Tarn

Garonne

Toulouse

Agour

Villefranche
de Lauragais

Mont-
giscard

Castelnaudary

Alzonne

Canal du Midi

Bézier

Ariège

Canal du Midi

Aude

Ag

Carcassonne

Narbonne

Limoux

Canal de la Robine

Foix

Port-
la-Nouve

Aude

Perpignan

Andorra

Spain

25 km

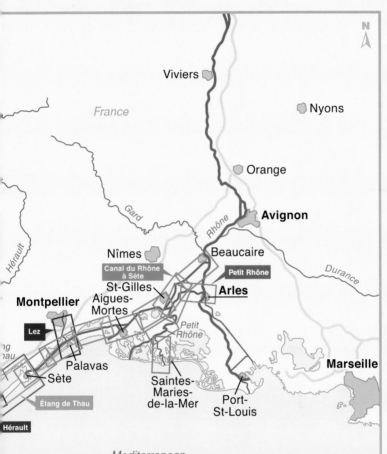

Viviers

Nyons

France

Orange

Avignon

Gard

Rhône

Hérault

Nîmes

Beaucaire

Canal du Rhône à Sète

Petit Rhône

Durance

St-Gilles

Arles

Montpellier

Aigues-Mortes

Lez

Petit Rhône

Marseille

Palavas

Sète

Saintes-Maries-de-la-Mer

Port-St-Louis

Étang de Thau

Hérault

Mediterranean

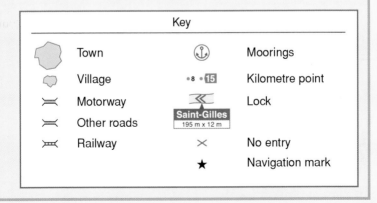

Key			
Town		Moorings	
Village		•8 •15 Kilometre point	
Motorway		Lock	
Other roads	Saint-Gilles 195 m x 12 m	No entry ×	
Railway		Navigation mark ★	

CLIMATE

With a mild climate and extended season, the region that includes the Canal du Midi and surrounding canals is the most popular in France for boat-hire. From March through to November you can rely on having mild weather. My own favourite is the month of May, when the plane trees are in leaf and the yellow irises are coming into bloom on the waterway banks. You may hear nightingales singing right through the night, and the call of the black and yellow oriole can be heard all day long.

NAVIGATING THE WATERWAYS

The southern French canal system is divided into two halves by the Étang de Thau. From Toulouse to Marseillan, 91 lock chambers have to be navigated. The countryside is hilly and there are many attractive views along the route. The locks are electrified all the way through, and a well-organised crew of two can easily manage to take on the challenge of the Canal du Midi. However, experience in throwing ropes and mooring, and in the proper (slow!) manoeuvring of the boat are all-important with only two on board. Ideally, three adults should be the minimum crew. Two-man crews with less experience, or those who find the number of locks tedious, should stay on the waters to the east of the Étang de Thau. In that area there are only three locks, which are all electrified, and a week's cruising can be planned to avoid having to pass through any locks. The countryside here is more monotonous but has the attraction that the sea is close by. In several places, the bathing beaches are not only within sight, but just five or ten minutes' walk away.

CHARTER COMPANIES

All the well-known boat-hire firms in France have established themselves on the Canal du Midi or in the surrounding area – some of them with two or even three bases. This means that one-way cruising is possible. Your car can be driven to meet you for a suitable fee, or you can travel back by railway at the end of the cruise to collect your vehicle.

The pioneering work on charter boats was done by the English company Blue Line from around the early 1970s on the Canal du Midi; they merged with Crown Cruisers to form Crown Blue Line. Another English company is Connoisseur Holidays Afloat. Crown Blue Line and Connoisseur are both within the First Choice group of companies which merged with the German company TUI Marine. Now based at Port Solent, Portsmouth, Crown Blue Line and Connoisseur advertise jointly as *Le Boat*. The French firms which are active nationwide are Rive de France, Locaboat and Nicols.

In the last few years the charter boat business has been transformed. Most of the larger firms have opened offices overseas, smaller agencies have become bigger or have had to close down – not least because of competition from direct bookings via the internet. This is regrettable, because some independent, specialist travel agents are able to provide impartial advice and help the customer to find the right boat in the right area. They had a loyal clientele and, as a rule, they provided the sort of personal attention that you do not always find with the mass tour operators. Because they work

Cruising the River Lez, south of Montpellier.

with several boat-hire companies, they have a larger selection of craft and almost always manage to find an available boat somewhere, even when the motor cruiser you had originally chosen is booked for your dates. Those who think they can book cheaper locally are mistaken, because the agencies book boats at the operators' prices and get their commission from the hire firm.

Being able to choose from over a thousand charter boats, you are really spoilt for choice. The guiding principle is always opt for one size bigger than you need! If possible, the saloon should not need to be converted in the evenings, to avoid disturbing people during the night and in the mornings. Don't forget, everybody will literally be in the same boat – crews have to be accommodated who may already find lack of space ashore a problem! Friction can be sparked off by trifling incidents, so everyone should have their own quiet place where they can go to chill out.

Lots of people already have the image of what their dream cruiser should look like. But a river boat is not designed to

Evening on the Étang de Thau.

cut through the waves. The somewhat ungainly bathtubs with a forward steering position and a foredeck for sunbathing are the boats probably best suited for a sociable family holiday. As all the cabins are on one level, this reduces the hazard of tripping on the stairs. Boats with the steering position amidships or in the stern are easier to steer since, unlike cars, the aft end swings out when altering course. The helmsman has a better overall view if the full length of the boat lies in front of him. Very popular now are boats with a second open steering position amidships on a 'flybridge'. From this vantage point the overall view and all-round visibility are excellent.

TOURISM

Many people want to spend some time ashore, either before or after their boat trip. In coastal towns in the south of France, which have been developed over the years, there are plenty of basic hotels for tourists. For those who wish to stay in more stylish accommodation in elegant surroundings among the locals, I recommend enquiring at the French Government Tourist Office for lists of rental villas, houses and flats. The address is: Maison de la France, 300 Lincoln House, High Holborn, London WC1V 7JH. Telephone 0906 824 4123. Website: www.franceguide.com.

Some people prefer to stay in a pretty hostel. *Le Guide des Hôtels-Restaurants* which is published annually by Logis de France, contains over 3000 independent inns and smaller, affordable hotels across France. With regard to prices, they compare favourably with the chains of motels sited on arterial roads and in industrial areas which seem to offer economic rates. With their uniform rooms and menus, the chain hotels tend to detract from the image of France as a nation of individualists who enjoy the pleasures of life. But on our last holiday on the Midi, we made a stop-over at the l'Ousteau Camarguen Hotel in Grau du Roi and can thoroughly recommend this three-star establishment as a cosy oasis in the midst of the hustle and bustle along the coast.

TECHNICAL DATA ON THE WATERWAYS

CANAL DU RHÔNE À SÈTE

Length: 98 km

Locks: 1, length 80m x width 5.20m

Draught: 2.20m between St Gilles and Sète;
1.80m between St Gilles and Beaucaire

Headroom: 5m between St Gilles and Sète;
4.10m between St Gilles and Beaucaire

Speed: up to 10kph

PETIT RHÔNE

Length: 20km to the St Gilles connecting canal;
from there 37km to Grau d'Orgon (for
charter boats the limit is 34km)

Locks: 1 on the St Gilles connecting canal,
length 195m x width 12m

Draught: 2.20m from Rhône to St Gilles connecting
canal; 0.70m from connecting canal to
the sea

Headroom: 4.70m between the Rhône and St Gilles
connecting canal; 2.50m between the
connecting canal and Sauvage ferry

LEZ

Length: 5km from Palavas as far as Lattes

Locks: 1, length 30m x width 5.20m

Draught: 1.5m

Headroom: 3.30m

ÉTANG DE THAU

Length: 17km between Sète and Les Onglous
lighthouse

Draught: Étang de Thau 2.00m; Marseillan 1.60m;
Mèze 2.50m; Bouzigues 2.50m

CANAL DU MIDI

Length: 240km
Locks: 63 (91 chambers), minimum length 30m
x width 5.60m
Draught: 1.40m
Headroom: 3.30m
Malpas tunnel: length 161m x width 6.45m x height 5m
Speed limit: 8kph

HÉRAULT

Length: 7km from Agde to Bessan; 5km from Agde
to le Grau d'Agde
Locks: 1, round lock in Agde
Draught: 1.50m between Agde and Bessan
2.90m between Agde and le Grau d'Agde
Headroom: no bridges between Agde and Bessan
4.10m between Agde and le Grau d'Agde

CANAL DE LA ROBINE

Length: 5km to Canal de Jonction (connecting
canal)
600m of the Aude 32km from
Moussoulens lock
to Port-la-Nouvelle (Canal de la Robine)
Locks: 7 – Canal de Jonction
6 – Canal de la Robine
length 40.50m x width 5.85m
Draught: 1.60m
Headroom: 3.30m
Speed limit: 8kph

WATERWAY VOCABULARY

accostage	alongside mooring	*digue*	dyke
amarrage	mooring	*duc d'albe*	mooring post
amasse	grouping of boats to enter lock	*échelle d'écluses*	staircase of locks
amont	upstream; upper reaches	*écluse*	lock
		éclusier, -ière	lock keeper
appontement	pontoon	*espar*	post used as navigation mark
aval	downstream; lower reaches	*halage*	towing
avalant	descending	*halte fluviale*	bankside mooring
avis à la batellerie	notice to boat owners	*haut fond*	shallows
bâbord	port side	*mouillage*	deep water for mooring
bac	cross-river ferry	*NNN*	guaranteed normal water level
bajoyer	lock wall		
barrage	weir/dam	*perche*	suspended rod turned to operate lock
batillage	boat's wash		
bief	stretch of water between two locks	*portes de garde*	lock gates used only in flood conditions
chemin de halage	tow-path		
chômage	period of closure of locks for maintenance	*radier*	bottom of a lock
		régulation	lock operation outside normal hours
clapot	small waves		
confluent	the meeting of two or more rivers	*sas*	lock chamber
		tirant d'air	air draught
		tirant d'eau	draught
darse	basin	*trémater*	overtake
délaissé	closed canal	*tribord*	starboard side
dérivation	section of canal bypassing a nearby river	*vantelle*	lock sluices

CANAL DU RHÔNE À SÈTE

Beaucaire is one of those southern French towns with a great history and was formerly a thriving trading centre, evidenced today by the distant view of the castle on the far side of the Rhône, the churches of St Paul and Notre Dame des Pommiers, and the 17th century town hall. Its past commercial importance is reflected in the ornate town houses once owned by wealthy merchants. From the 13th century, this was one of Europe's most important markets, attracting traders from all over Europe. Today, the little town with its population of 13,000, quietly sleeps beside the Rhône. The entrance to the Canal du Rhône à Sète from the Rhône has been closed off for years, so Beaucaire does not benefit from its location close to the great shipping route. The canal harbour has become a cul-de-sac.

The road bridge here, spanning the Rhône, carries heavy traffic to and from Tarascon on the east bank. Those who

The busy harbour at Beaucaire has plenty of facilities.

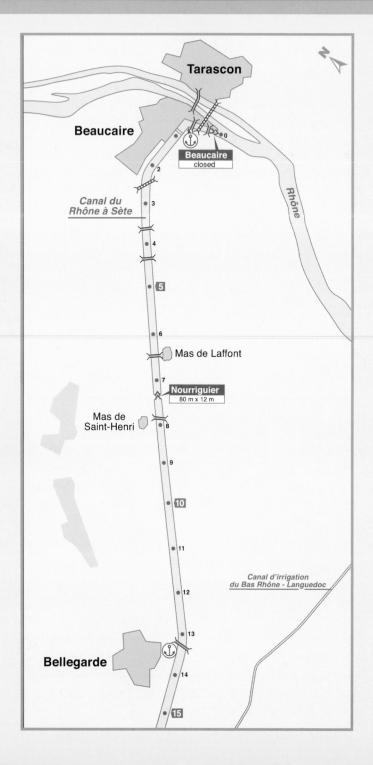

Tarascon

Beaucaire

Rhône

2

Canal du
Rhône à Sète

3

4

5

6

Mas de Laffont

7

Nourriguier
80 m x 12 m

Mas de
Saint-Henri

8

9

10

11

Canal d'irrigation
du Bas Rhône - Languedoc

12

13

Bellegarde

14

15

Beaucaire
closed

The lock at Nourriguier is self-operating.

fancy a 15-minute walk from the harbour can cross the bridge to visit Tarascon's magnificent castle.

At one time the Rhône formed the frontier between the regions of the Counts of Toulouse and those of Provence. Tarascon is similar in size to Beaucaire, and both are made up of alleys originally designed for pedestrians and donkeys, and not for cars.

BEAUCAIRE

The harbour at Beaucaire, located in the middle of town, has been converted from a commercial port to a harbour for pleasure boats. Quays for larger boats have been renovated and planted with trees and flowers, and pontoons provided for smaller craft. The pines and the café in the shade of leafy plane trees certainly give the impression of a colourful Mediterranean harbour lacking just one thing – direct access to the Rhône and thus a shorter route to the open sea. For

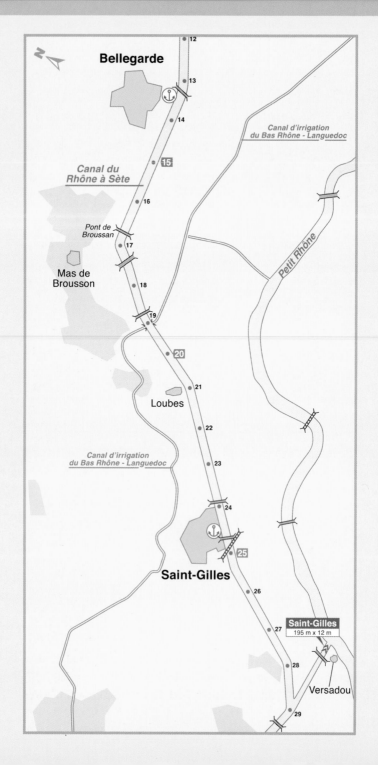

years there have been plans to re-open the out-of-service lock, which would make the town very popular with pleasure boaters and would also link the harbour with the sailing school on an enclosed side river where weirs now prevent through-navigation.

When the harbour was rebuilt, a lifting footbridge was provided across the basin which, when raised, provides 5.5m clearance.

The Maison de Tourisme is located right next to this bridge. For good-value regional cooking, the *Michelin Guide* recommends Les Vignes Blanches and L'Oliverai, both of them on the road to Nîmes. There are shops in the town centre only a short walk from the harbour for those who prefer to dine on board.

It is worth mentioning that from Beaucaire it is only 20 kilometres to the world-famous Pont du Gard, the impressive remains of the Roman 3-tiered aqueduct

Hire cruisers tied up on the moorings near the town of Bellegarde.

extending from the hills to Nîmes. On the way there, about two kilometres outside Beaucaire, stands the 'Robinson' inn, an oasis of peace with beautifully landscaped gardens and play areas for children. The triangle between Avignon, Arles and Nîmes, is a poplar area to search for holiday homes. The Robinson and L'Oliverai are inns listed in the *Logis-de-France*.

Some boaters consider that the harbour at Beaucaire is unsuitable for overnight stops because of the traffic noise, and so are obliged to chug on for at least four kilometres out of town until the cement factory and other industrial sites are left behind. On the way you will pass a hire-boat base. You can make passage to more peaceful surroundings in the evening as the first and only lock on the canal route to Sète is seven kilometres from Beaucaire. This lock at Nourriguier, 80 metres long and 12 metres wide, is of modern construction and electrified. In order to activate the gates and paddles, a member of the crew needs only to push a single button in the

The canal between Bellegarde and St Gilles is a fairly straight run.

little control house; so it is very easy to operate. The 4-metre change in water level takes place very gently.

Between Beaucaire and St Gilles, the canal runs between thickly overgrown banks which are rarely cut back by the canal maintenance crews. There is hardly any commercial shipping on this stretch as the majority of the barges approaching from the west turn off before St Gilles to enter the Petit Rhône. Beyond the thick hedgerows and shrubs bordering the waterway, lie many hectares of fruitful vineyards.

At the bridge of Bellegarde, at the end of a long straight stretch of some 12 kilometres, there are moorings on both sides of the canal. The quay on the north side bears the name of Pierre-Paul Riquet, who designed and built the Canal du Midi in the 17th century. Here the visitor can find a restaurant, the harbour master's office, a hire-boat base and a toilet block. The quay opposite is named after Paulin Talabot, a less famous engineer who lived between 1799 and 1885 and planned the Canal du

Palm trees add a flavour of the south of France in St Gilles Port de Plaisance.

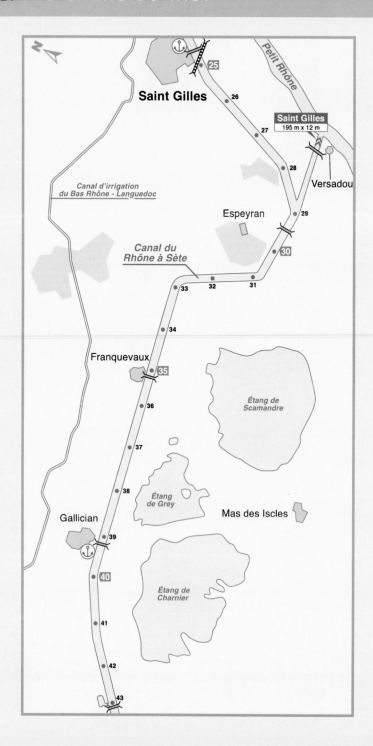

N

Saint Gilles

Petit Rhône

25

26

27

Saint Gilles
195 m x 12 m

28

Versadou

*Canal d'irrigation
du Bas Rhône - Languedoc*

Espeyran

29

*Canal du
Rhône à Sète*

30

33   32   31

34

Franquevaux

35

*Étang de
Scamandre*

36

37

*Étang
de Grey*

38

Mas des Iscles

Gallician

39

40

*Étang de
Charnier*

41

42

43

Rhône à Sète. In the centre of the village is a good selection of shops. Bellegarde is surrounded by vineyards and half way along the path to the village you will find a wine co-operative where you can stop for a wine-tasting session.

ST GILLES

Twenty-four kilometres along the canal from Beaucaire, is St Gilles. This town, too, has a long history, with its heyday in the Middle Ages when the town had four times as many inhabitants as it does today. The Roman façade of the church is authentic, but the sarcophagus with the bones of Saint Giles, after whom the town was named, is not.

The little town makes a very lively impression with many bars and restaurants and shops on the busy main street, which starts right at the canal harbour. The quays are packed with private boats and those from a hire-boat base, so that it is not at all easy at times to get a berth here. It is a convenient mooring for shopping and dining out, but the view across

Pleasure boaters are not the only ones who enjoy river views on the Canal du Rhône à Sète.

the water is of an disused distillery which, with sparkling, silvery pipework inadequately hidden behind slow-growing pines, gives the appearance of an oil refinery. It is not exactly a picturesque sight, but reminds us that canals were not built for tourism, but for economic reasons. Silos and factories constructed by the waterways are rarely marvels of architecture.

Beyond the heavily-used road bridge, the quay continues, overlooked by a wine storage facility. But after another 4 kilometres, on the left-hand side, the branch off towards the Petit Rhône comes into view. From here onwards, you have to expect to meet the occasional barge making passage between the Rhône and Sète.

COMMERCIAL WATERWAY TRAFFIC

A whole chapter could be easily devoted to the growth and decline of commercial traffic on the waterways, with nostalgic memories of the bargees. It is now rare to see a fully-loaded barge between Arles and Toulouse. Since the extensive widening of the waterway from the Rhône to the Mediterranean port of Sète (there is still a 9-kilometre long narrow section east of Carnon), commercial shipping has increased again somewhat. However, there are hardly any *péniches* here, which are the traditional canal boats with a length of just under 40 metres, but instead very much larger freighters. Due to the narrowness of the channel, in places they can move at only 6 kilometres per hour or less. For these vessels, Sète is the end of the line, and for the *péniches*, it is Béziers.

A law was passed in 1907 which caused all French locks to be lengthened to 40 metres, but these improvements did not extend to the locks between Béziers and Ayguesvives, 20 kilometres south of Toulouse. There remains a long gap in the improvement plan with lock chambers along most of the Midi being still only 30 metres long, which was Pierre-Paul Riquet's original specification way back in 1663; these are too short to accommodate the modern *péniche*. The sporadic water shortages on the canal in the early 1990s meant that the plans for deepening and lengthening the locks were shelved – to the disappointment of the owners of the few remaining *péniches* restricted to a short length of the Midi.

The postponed enlargement of Riquet's locks on the Midi was only one reason for the decline in barge traffic. The bargees could not compete with road and rail transport. In the 19th century, those involved in water transport did take up the challenge on the Canal du Midi and the Étang de Thau, providing a mail boat between Toulouse and Sète which achieved an average speed of 11 kilometres per hour. The mail boats operated day and night, changing the horses that pulled the barges every 8 kilometres. Diesel engines replaced the teams of horses in the 1930s, when barges would chug along at almost the same pace as the boatmen achieved in earlier times, hauling their craft along the waterway.

With the decline in canal transport, some owners have converted their *péniches* into passenger boats. There are three types of these conversions – floating restaurants for one-day excursions, barges equipped with dormitories used for childrens' holidays, and well-appointed craft in which small parties of guests are lavishly entertained at considerable expense. On occasions a minibus follows these cruise boats to enable guests to explore ashore. So these converted barges still provide a living for the boatmen, and enable some of them to continue what may have been a family tradition of working on the waterways for several generations.

Sometimes the sight of the hotel barges, five metres wide and three metres high, can be alarming when they suddenly appear round a narrow bend, and appear to be heading straight for you. Some of these bargees on the Midi are reluctant to be overtaken by other boats in case they grab the last space in a lock (particularly if it is close to lock-closing

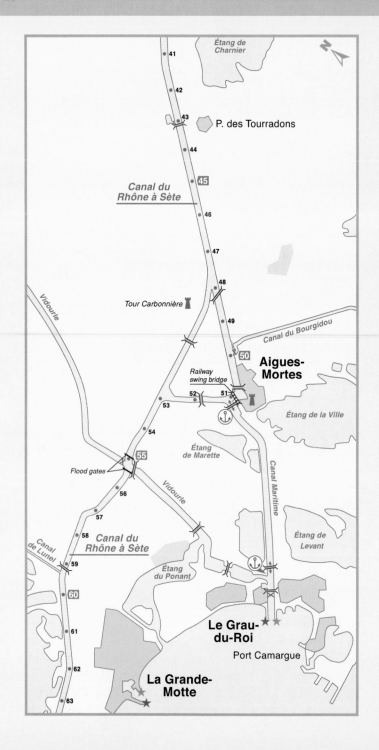

41

42

43

P. des Tourradons

Étang de Charnier

44

45

Canal du Rhône à Sète

46

47

48

Tour Carbonnière

49

Canal du Bourgidou

50

Aigues-Mortes

Railway swing bridge

52   51

53

Étang de la Ville

54

Étang de Marette

55

Flood gates

Vidourle

56

57

58   *Canal du Rhône à Sète*

Étang du Ponant

Étang de Levant

Canal de Lunel

59

Canal Maritime

60

61

Le Grau-du-Roi ★★

62

Port Camargue

63

La Grande-Motte

Vidourle

Moorings at Gallician.

time), making the hotel barge wait outside and upsetting their busy schedule.

The Canal du Rhône à Sète only has the one lock (Nourriguier) and lacks the attractive varied countryside which has made the Canal du Midi so popular with pleasure boats. During the upgrading of the waterway to carry larger vessels, the overgrown banks were cleared and embankments built up with stone and sand. The canal also extends across a flat featureless landscape beside lagoons and marshland but you may catch glimpses of flocks of exotic pink flamingos sifting the water for brine shrimps and other water creatures. You may also see fishermen on the lagoons (called *étangs*) wading around in the knee-deep water, gathering mussels and oysters.

Shortly after the junction of the connecting canal linking the Petit Rhône with the old canal to St Gilles and Beaucaire, the Espeyran bridge crosses the water, carrying the road to the nearby castle of Espeyran which has an impressive pine forest as a backdrop; like most of the castles in the region, it can only be admired from a distance. This bridge is a convenient place to view the marshes on both sides of the canal. From here, with a good pair of binoculars, you may well see grey heron and rarer bird species.

If you moor just a couple of hundred metres further on, near the tamarisk bushes and the six-foot high flowering thistles, at twilight you can enjoy a frog chorus of such an intensity that is rarely heard anywhere else in Central Europe. Hundreds if not thousands of frogs join in, creating a cacophony of sound, accompanied by a variety of birdsong. At around 10pm peace returns, until about midnight when you may be lucky enough to hear nightingales singing.

The Canal du Rhône à Sète, with sections that are motorway-straight for kilometres, is an excellent waterway for introducing the novice crew to the basics of boat handling. Those unfamiliar with the wheel of a boat may well be surprised how difficult it is to maintain a straight

A very straight section of the canal east of Aigues-Mortes.

course. Between Beaucaire and Bellegarde there is an eleven-kilometre dead straight section to negotiate, and west of St Gilles are six more kilometres with not even a gentle bend where you pass beneath the two bridges of Franquevaux and Gallician. Both villages lie within sight of the canal and have shops for basic essentials. At Gallician, there is a well-equipped yacht harbour near a wine cellar where you can sample the local wines.

Anglers are much in evidence in these parts, particularly under Gallician's bridge which provides shelter from sun and rain. They are not especially friendly to those who motor by in boats who, in the process, occasionally collect someone's fishing tackle round their propellers. For harmony on the waterways, give their lines a wide berth.

Ahead, the impressive Constance Tower of Aigues-Mortes comes into view, although still 8 kilometres away at the end of another dead straight section of canal. Amongst the

The railway swing bridge at Aigues-Mortes.

tamarisk and other bushes on the east bank, herds of the famous white Camargue horses can be seen. These animals roam freely but are not tame and will not allow themselves to be either fed or stroked.

About two and a half kilometres before Aigues-Mortes, the waterway splits into two. To the right, a detour built in 1994, bypasses Aigues-Mortes. This branch canal, cut through the sand on which the well-known Vin de Sable flourishes, is mainly for the benefit of commercial craft enabling them to avoid the congestion and bridges of Aigues-Mortes. Pleasure boats making for Aigues-Mortes and le Grau-du-Roi continue straight ahead.

The 13th century Constance tower at Aigues-Mortes.

AIGUES-MORTES

Umbrella pine trees line the banks of the canal in the outskirts of Aigues-Mortes. In the entrance to a blocked-off side canal, a couple of old *péniches* have been laid up. Beyond, in the town's basin, the quays are packed with boats of all shapes and sizes, making it difficult for the visitor to find anywhere to moor up, even for a short stay to take on provisions. Leaving the basin may involve waiting for the railway swing bridge to open, although this is rare because railway traffic to and from le Grau-du-Roi on the coast is modest. Traffic lights are displayed by the bridge which closes ten minutes before the arrival of a train. After the railway bridge, it is a 90° turn to port into the Chenal maritime to gain access to the town's over-crowded *port de plaisance*. With restricted space for visiting boats, the best bet to explore Aigues-Mortes may be to continue on to le Grau-du-Roi and berth here for the night, returning to Aigues-Mortes to sightsee by train, bus or taxi (5 kilometres).

The town of Aigues-Mortes owes its existence to King Louis IX's passion for riches of the Orient. Travel and pillaging were disguised under the respectable banner of Crusading, and he was eventually made a saint. God evidently had a different perspective, for during his second Crusade in 1270, Louis IX became a victim of the plague, and never returned to France.

Nevertheless, Louis IX's legacy was the town of Aigues-Mortes. Surrounded by well-preserved ramparts impressively illuminated after dark, the old town attracts hordes of tourists. The king's statue stands in Place St Louis, where you can enjoy a peaceful drink in the evening when the day-trippers have returned home. Some consider that Aigues-Mortes is the most impressive place to moor up between Toulouse and Arles.

Through the centuries, this port suffered from silting up, like the neighbouring inland ports of Narbonne and Agde, and is now some 6 kilometres from the sea. The Chenal Maritime

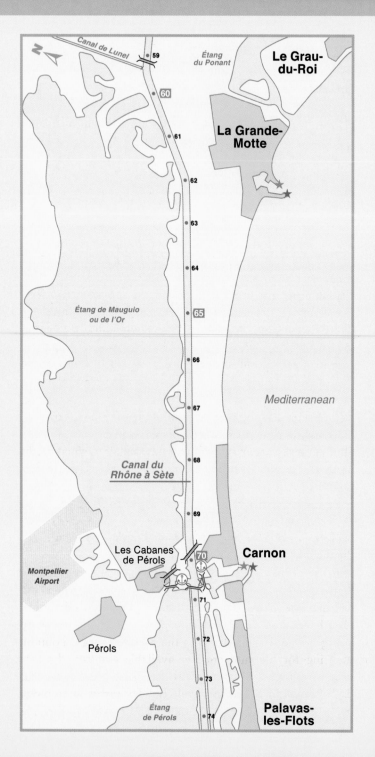

At le Grau-du-Roi there is access to the Mediterranean Sea.

between Aigues-Mortes and le Grau-du-Roi can be negotiated by boats with a maximum draught of 1.10 metres and a height above waterline of no more than 2.4 metres. If the boat height is more than 2.4 metres, the bridgemaster at le Grau-du-Roi will have to be contacted at the downstream swing bridge which links the two halves of this busy seaside resort. If you reckon you will need the services of le Grau-du-Roi's bridgemaster, it is advisable to ask for his telephone number at the office of Aigues-Mortes' harbour master.

The seaward swing bridge at le Grau-du-Roi is continually in operation to allow the fishing boats to leave and return. Hire boats are not permitted to pass through this seaward swing bridge to gain access to the Mediterranean. Pontoon mooring for pleasure craft is available between the two bridges, opposite the fishing harbour. What was a somewhat drab fishing port is now a lively holiday resort, with many bars and restaurants overlooking the picturesque quays occupied by colourful working craft. In the entrance stands a lighthouse and to the south the vast maritime marina development of Port-Camargue.

VIDOURLE RIVER

Those boats whose skippers have made the recommended detour to spend the night at le Grau-du-Roi have, in theory, a choice of routes back to the Canal du Rhône à Sète. Opposite the pontoon berths is the entrance to the River Vidourle which leads back to the canal, but the depth in the river invariably rules this out as an option and there are two fixed bridges (headroom 2.80 metres and 3.50 metres). The only alternative is to backtrack to Aigues-Mortes turning up the western branch canal to port just after the first of the town's bridges (approaching from le Grau-du-Roi). This 2.5-kilometre branch canal from Aigues-Mortes, to re-join the Canal du Rhône à Sète, is one-way traffic. It is regulated according to a time-table which is prominently displayed on the bankside notice mounted in the entrance to the branch canal.

The River Vidourle flood gates.

Canal du Rhône à Sète

Étang de Pérols

● 73

● 74

[75] ●

Lez

● 76

Palavas-les-Flots

Étang du Prévost

● 77

Étang de l'Arnel

● 78

Floating footbridge

● 79

Maguelone

Maguelone Cathedral (ruin)

[80] ●

Villeneuve- les-Maguelone

● 81

Étang de Pierre Blanche

● 82

Mediterranean

Étang des Moures

● 83

● 84

Canal du Rhône à Sète

Mireval

[85] ●

Étang de Vic

✕ ● 86

les Aresquiers

● 87

Vic-la-Gardiole

● 88

Mooring can sometimes be difficult alongside eroded banks.

A hire cruiser keeps out of the way of a large barge where the canal narrows near Carnon.

Having re-joined the Canal du Rhône à Sète and proceeding westwards, you pass two pairs of flood gates positioned where the River Vidourle crosses the canal. These gates are lowered to protect the canal when the river is in flood. A few kilometres beyond the Vidourle crossing, the canal has been built on a narrow sand spit extending 30 kilometres all the way to Sète. To the north is a series of *étangs* or brackish lagoons; to the south is the Mediterranean with popular bathing beaches and more lagoons.

There is insufficient height from the deck of a pleasure boat to glimpse the Mediterranean but the unmistakable towering pyramid-shaped blocks of apartments of la Grande-Motte with its vast maritime marina give you an indication of how close you are to the coastline. On the other side of the canal, former fishermen's huts at Cabanes du Roc break up a somewhat bleak watery landscape.

For the next 9 kilometres as far as Carnon, the canal has not been widened to carry commercial craft. There are very few barges these days above Sète, but if you are unlucky enough to meet one you can't just steer the boat into the bank to avoid a scrape or a fierce wash. If you do spot an approaching barge, the locals advise retreating back to Cabanes du Roc or Carnon and wait there to allow the vessel to pass by.

CARNON-PLAGE

Carnon is a popular holiday resort with long beaches. Past the first of Carnon's road bridges is a hire-boat base on the seaward side. The harbour on the same side, just before the second road bridge, is for small local boats only as the fixed bridge in the entrance has just 1.20 metres of headroom. To starboard is a specially constructed harbour with a long row of mooring posts for pleasure boats. This harbour is part of the connecting canal from the Étang de Mauguio or Étang de l'Or to the Mediterranean, in which, depending on the wind direction and the time of day there can be a strong current. Contrary to popular belief, the Mediterranean does have

Former fishermen's huts on the canalside are now used as weekend cottages.

modest tides, with a difference in levels of perhaps 20 to 30 centimetres along this stretch of coast. Before attempting to berth in this narrow waterway, less than 20 metres across, you should carefully observe the current and the wind direction. When entering or leaving here, pay attention to the strong cross-current which has driven more than one inexperienced skipper against the low bridge, under which the water streams towards the sea. If you also have to cope with a strong wind, getting free without assistance can be quite a job.

PARADISE FOR ANGLERS

Fishermen populate the banks of the canal both during the day and through the night when they provide an attractive spectacle with their luminous red and green floats. Others search by torchlight for shellfish amongst the rocks. At dusk another spectacle is occasionally provided by hundreds of flamingos in flight overhead, making their way from one *étang* to another.

For those who want to sample the entertainment in Carnon-Plage, it is something of an assault-course from the moorings on the north side of the canal, crossing two bridges and then skirting round the maritime marina to reach the centre of Carnon Est.

Five kilometres west of Carnon is the holiday resort, fishing harbour and maritime marina of Palavas-les-Flots. The Canal du Rhône à Sète does not pass it directly because the Étang du Grec and the Étang du Prevost are in between. Palavas-les-Flots is actually in the mouth of the River Lez where it runs into the Mediterranean. The Lez crosses the canal with a current similar to that experienced at Carnon, but less hazardous because there is ample head room beneath the bridge over the Lez. This must be negotiated to reach the town's moorings in the Pierre-Paul Riquet *port de plaisance* which you share with sand yachts and mobile homes. Cross the first of the town bridges to reach the Étang du Grec for a close-up view of flamingos. The town offers plenty of entertainment with a large selection of restaurants, a fine beach and a casino.

A pleasant excursion in these parts is to take the boat along the upstream section of the River Lez which is navigable for

Flamingos are a frequent sight along
the Canal du Rhône à Sète.

The crowded port de plaisance at
Palavas-les-Flots.

5 kilometres to Port Ariane marina (see pages 61-2). The next
landmark along this somewhat featureless canal route among
the *étangs* are the ruins of the Cathedral of Maguelonne. This
was built on an island surrounded by water and sand, and
until the 11th century the cathedral could only be reached by
boat. The canal, at this point, can only be crossed by means
of a floating footbridge which, when in use, can be opened
for canal traffic in response to a hoot on the horn. Those in
boats wanting to visit the ruin or bathe in the nearby sea can
moor up either side of the bridge. If the mistral is blowing
hard from the land towards the sea, a boat with a tall
superstructure and a low-powered engine, can find casting off
from the downstream moorings on the south bank difficult.

More moorings convenient for the beach are another 6
kilometres along the canal at Mas d'Angoulême on the south
bank, a kilometre upstream of les Aresquiers bridge. It is
virtually impossible to moor up nearer to the bridge because
local boats occupy all the space in front of the neat rows of
houses, which is a pity because it is only a short walk from
the bridge to the beach – part of which is reserved for nudists.

The quays of Palavas-les-Flots with the Mediterranean beyond.

FRONTIGNAN

The canal now takes you towards Frontignan which is 5 kilometres away. The silhouette of this town was for years dominated by a giant refinery which has now been closed down and dismantled. Only the huge tanks still stand. Most pleasure craft will be obliged to stop for a while at Frontignan because the canal is spanned by a low lifting road bridge which, during the season, is only raised three times a day during the week and twice over weekends (Mon-Fri 0700, 1300, 1630; Sat-Sun 0900, 1700). These opening times can be checked by reference to the schedule displayed on the cabin of the bridge master. Sète-bound downstream traffic has priority. Have the boat all ready for slipping well before the opening time, for the traffic rushes through like the start of a powerboat race, and the bridge master does not wait for dawdlers. Commercial craft avoid the lifting bridge by turning off to port just before Frontignan, taking the side canal (closed to pleasure boats unsuitable for maritime conditions) that leads to the fishing harbour and the open sea. In Frontignan, the quayside, once occupied by barges, has been smartened up for the use of pleasure boats. A sign indicates a maximum stay of 24 hours, but many boat owners

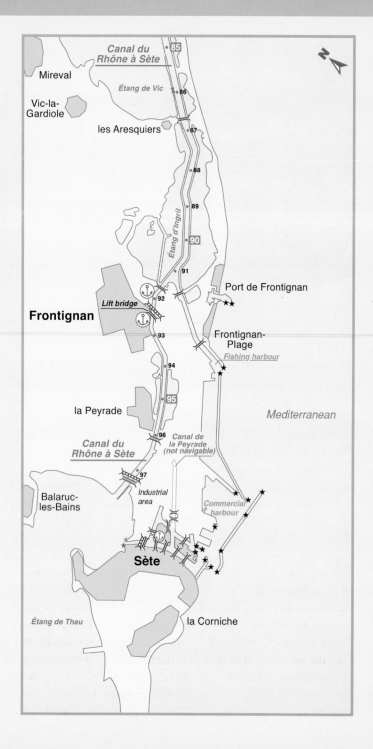

Frontignan's lifting road bridge.

seem to ignore this, using the town quay as a permanent berth. In the past Frontignan was considered to be a down-market bathing beach, perhaps because of the view of the oil refinery. This has all changed and the holiday resort suburb of Frontignan-Plage with its large maritime marina, can compete with the best of the neighbouring seaside resorts. Those who do not fancy the 2-kilometre hike to Frontignan-Plage, can stroll around the old part of the town which has several wine cellars, a remarkable fortified church and a good selection of shops. At La Marine restaurant you will find good regional food at reasonable prices.

The route from Frontignan to the entrance into the Étang de Thau near Sète is lined with the oil tanks previously mentioned on the seaward side; opposite, a small lagoon has been transformed into a recreational area. Beyond, the industrial sprawl reaches down to both sides of the canal. At the end of the canal is a small red beacon tower – an important navigation mark to be identified by skippers of craft coming in the opposite direction, looking for the entrance to the Canal du Rhône à Sète. Having reached the

Seagulls in the air indicate that the sea is close by.

red day mark motoring west, craft either turn south and take the well-marked channel to the inland entrance to the port of Sète or continue westwards into the Étang de Thau, making for the substantial beacon towers (yellow and black and red and black). The bay on the seaward side between the red spar beacon and the beacon towers is shallow.

Canals run through the centre of Sète, some suitable only for small craft.

SÈTE

Sète is one of the largest French ports for both commercial shipping and fishing, where craft of every size from rowing-boats to ocean-going giants are on the move. So if up until now you have only cruised on comparatively tranquil canals and rivers, you may find entering Sète a challenging experience. Having cleared the entrance marked with red and green light towers, there are berths alongside the quay immediately to port. If you want a more permanent berth in the marina, this involves waiting for the daily opening (usually at 10.00 hours) of the substantial rail and road bridges to gain access to the large basin opposite the railway station, which accommodates a marina and quayside berths right in the centre of the town.

If the Canal du Midi was not proof enough of Pierre-Paul Riquet's genius, the town of Sète certainly is. Riquet insisted on creating a new maritime port at the foot of Mont St Clair, accessible from his Canal du Midi by way of the Étang de Thau and defying the silting up that most of the neighbouring Mediterranean harbours have had to contend with. The 300-year-old town of Sète, by contrast, has to this

day the sea literally on its doorstep. Where else would you find, for instance, an enormous car ferry to Morocco moored in the centre of the town?

With a population of 40,000, Sète is not a large town, but well able to avoid the economic downturn of other ports. At present, they are trying to expand tourism in the town. The sandbar between the Étang de Thau and the Mediterranean is still largely unexploited, and will probably remain that way. It carries the railway and a trunk road, leaving little land for further development. Tourists come to Sète mostly during the day from the beaches in the vicinity. From Frontignan, where you can leave your boat moored up for the day, Sète is only one stop on the train. The first impression of the town is that it consists solely of the harbour, but the visitor will also discover an abundance of art galleries, museums, theatres and cinemas. There is a vast choice of restaurants, and if you don't mind forgoing the views of fishing boats and fishermen mending their nets, you may find a better-value menu a couple of streets away.

At the end of the Canal du Rhône à Sète is a small red beacon tower ... and a notice with information about navigating the Étang de Thau.

PETIT RHÔNE

Some boaters prefer canals, others favour rivers which are mostly broader, following a course dictated by the landscape unless diverted by man-made dams or weirs or by channel dredging. The advantage of canals is that they are mostly navigable across their entire width, unless a collapsed bank has created shallows where reeds and water lilies warn the skipper to keep a safe distance off the bank and into deeper water.

In the south of France there are not many opportunities to cruise on free-flowing waters such as the Rhône, prefixed 'Grand' in order to distinguish it from the Petit Rhône, as well as stretches of the Vidourle, Lez, Hérault and Aude. Only a boat with suitable engine capacity can take on the Grand Rhône's sometimes fierce current. Most hire-boats have regulated engines limiting the top speed to 10 kilometres per hour so their skippers have no opportunity to try their hand at power-boating. With this lack of power,

Camargue horses grazing beside the Petit Rhône.

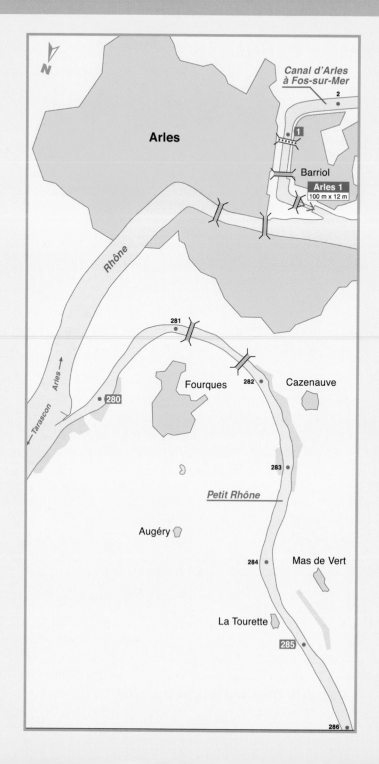

Canal d'Arles
à Fos-sur-Mer

2

1

Arles

Barriol

Arles 1
100 m x 12 m

Rhône

281

Arles →

Fourques

282

Cazenauve

← Tarascon

280

283

Petit Rhône

Augéry

284

Mas de Vert

La Tourette

285

286

hire-boats would find it difficult to cope with strong wind against current conditions, and are not licensed to navigate the Grand Rhône.

The current in the Petit Rhône, in normal conditions, is perfectly manageable. The river branches westwards from the Rhône just upstream of Arles and after 57 kilometres empties into the Mediterranean at Stes Maries-de-la-Mer. From the junction with the Rhône as far as the turning off to the St Gilles lock (20 kilometres), the channel is marked with port and starboard buoys, indicating a minimum depth in the channel of 2.2 metres in normal conditions. Distances can be read off from big column-like markers on the river bank. They start at 280 at the Rhône end and continue to 299 just before the entrance channel to St Gilles lock. This marking system is quite helpful, although some of the signs are completely obscured by vegetation, and there are few other clues on the banks of the Petit Rhône to help you fix your position.

The embankments on both sides of the river have a dense growth of bushes and tall trees, impenetrable by eye or on foot. Mooring is very difficult, even in an emergency, and downstream of the navigation buoys, beyond the turn off to the St Gilles lock, lie unmarked sandbanks. This is the reason why most hire-boat firms forbid their customers to venture into the Petit Rhône or they put them off by warning of the problems likely to be encountered.

Experienced skippers motoring slow ahead and continuously sounding the depth – even if reduced to probing with the boathook – will make it to the bank, where they will moor up with extra long lines to allow for a pronounced overnight increase or decrease in the water level. Anyone who has witnessed the inexperienced skipper on the Petit Rhône, struggling with the steering and the throttle, will have some sympathy for the hire-boat operator's restrictions. Moreover, in the event of a breakdown, their service vehicles will have a job reaching the boat because a towpath along the Petit Rhône is non-existent.

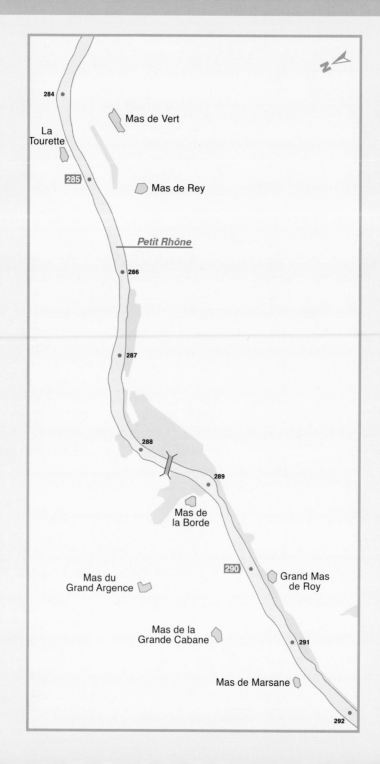

284

Mas de Vert

La
Tourette

285

Mas de Rey

Petit Rhône

286

287

288

289

Mas de
la Borde

290

Mas du
Grand Argence

Grand Mas
de Roy

Mas de la
Grande Cabane

291

Mas de Marsane

292

Bridges to help you identify your position are not exactly plentiful – two road bridges leading to Arles between Km 281 and 282, the A 54 – E 80 motorway bridge between Km 288 and 289, a railway bridge between Km 294 and 295, the National Trunk Road N 572 bridge near St Gilles between Km 297 and 298, and finally, way downriver, the Sylveréal road bridge 16 kilometres from the sea.

Some 2 kilometres downstream from the Trunk Road N 572 bridge, the entrance to St Gilles lock comes into view. The lock is situated in a short 2-kilometre stretch of canal linking the Petit Rhône with the Canal du Rhône à Sète. The lock's chamber is built to standard Rhône dimensions (195 x 12 metres), and even the skippers of large vessels feel somewhat lost when the giant gates close behind them. The lock is, of course, electrified. It is controlled from an elevated tower. The man up at the top makes his presence known to crews by light and hand signals. Red means stop, green means motor in, hand signals mostly *bonjour* or *au revoir*. The lift in the lock is normally modest, depending on the water level

The bridge by St Gilles lock.

of the Petit Rhône. Securing in the chamber presents no problems. Even after flooding when the rise/fall may be over 2 metres, there are no worries about turbulence as this is achieved without so much as a ripple on the surface.

Those who arrive to find the gates shut, need not risk approaching the steep embankments to land someone. On each side of the lock, three mooring platforms in suitably deep water have been built, and the middle one is connected to the bank by a gangway. Mooring overnight here is not recommended as a barge might arrive in the evening seeking the berth because the lock keeper has finished for the day. In any case, the somewhat bleak surroundings do not exactly encourage a stop-over. This connecting canal was built where the two waterways converge, and the nearest civilisation is St Gilles which is 5 kilometres from the lock.

For those in their own boats who wish to navigate the remaining 37 kilometres of the Petit Rhône as far as the Mediterranean (hire-boats are not permitted beyond the

Sylvéréal bridge.

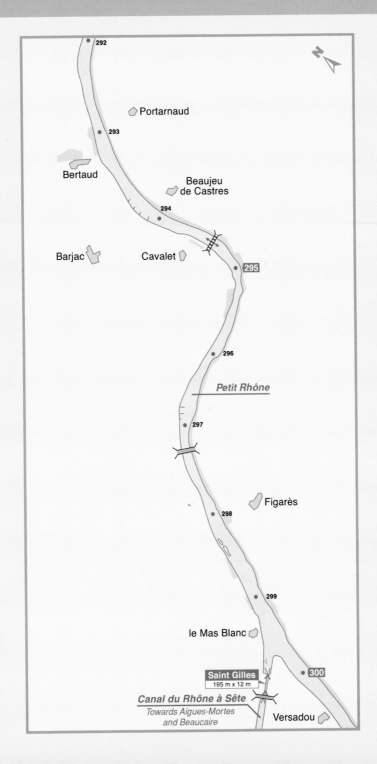

292

Portarnaud

293

Bertaud

Beaujeu
de Castres

294

Barjac

Cavalet

295

296

Petit Rhône

297

Figarès

298

299

le Mas Blanc

Saint Gilles
195 m x 12 m

300

Canal du Rhône à Sête
Towards Aigues-Mortes
and Beaucaire

Versadou

Sauvage ferry), the surroundings are equally bleak, with the banks of the river still covered with dense growth, and no buoys marking the extensive shallows (the official depth for the section of the river is quoted as only 0.7 metres). Kilometre distance marks are still on the bank to Km 331, just past the ferry at Sauvage, but they are frequently obscured by vegetation. To keep track of the boat's progress, on the map tick off the bends in the meandering river after rounding them. The channel is mostly in the middle of the river, but keep to the outside of bends to avoid the sandbanks on the inside.

Nobody with a boat drawing more than 70 centimetres should attempt this section of the Petit Rhône below the entrance to the St Gilles lock. Those who do nose into this waterway and, in spite of prudent navigation, still manage to run aground, may be able to re-float the boat by going full astern. If this does not work, somebody will have to get into the water and push. If a shallow-draught boat has grounded, generally speaking an adult will find firm enough footing

Sauvage ferry – end of river navigation for hire-boats.

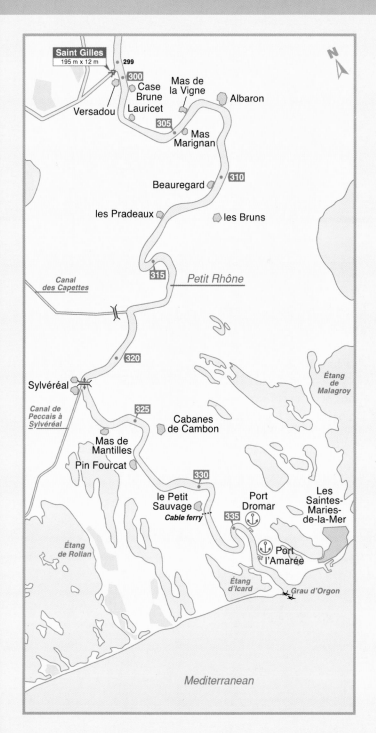

Saint Gilles
195 m x 12 m
• 299
300
Case Brune Lauricet
Mas de la Vigne
Albaron
Versadou
305
Mas Marignan
310
Beauregard
les Pradeaux
les Bruns
315
Canal des Capettes
Petit Rhône
320
Sylvéréal
Canal de Peccais à Sylvéréal
Étang de Malagroy
325
Cabanes de Cambon
Mas de Mantilles
Pin Fourcat
330
le Petit Sauvage
Cable ferry
Port Dromar
335
Les Saintes-Maries-de-la-Mer
Port l'Amarée
Étang de Rollan
Étang d'Icard
Grau d'Orgon
Mediterranean

to push the boat into deep water. Lifejackets as a safety precaution are a good idea, and using a safety line is recommended bearing in mind that the Petit Rhône is a river, although the current under normal conditions is usually no more than 2 kilometres per hour.

The Petit Rhône does not pass by any built-up areas, so there are no opportunities to provision the boat en route. At Km 324, the Sylvéréal bridge carries the main road across the river. Yacht skippers with thoughts of hoisting their masts after the bridge in anticipation of reaching the open sea should note that 9 kilometres further on, a ferry crosses the river by means of a steel cable which is suspended at a height of only 2.5 metres above the water.

Seven kilometres beyond the Sauvage ferry is the open sea. Underpowered and unstable to cope with the Mediterranean's wind and waves, the ferry marks the end of the line for those in hire-boats who have been authorised to navigate the Petit Rhône (at the other end of the river, the Fourques suspension bridge, within a kilometre of the Grand Rhône, is the limit for hire-boats).

RIVER LEZ

The River Lez is 30 kilometres long and flows south from the hills north of Montpellier, emptying into the Mediterranean at Palavas-les-Flots. From the 17th century it was navigable with the aid of three locks; around 1940, commercial shipping on the river ceased. Because of the brisk waterway traffic on the southern French waterways in the late 1980s, it was planned to make the Lez, which crosses the Canal du Rhône à Sète just upstream of Palavas-les-Flots, navigable again.

The little river winds through countryside where storks can be seen on their nests as you motor by. If you wonder why neither the storks nor the flamingos have fallen prey to hunters, apparently the flesh of both bird species is unpalatable.

The first structure along the Lez to be renovated was Troisième lock, about 5 kilometres inland. It is built in the distinctive oval shape like the locks on the Canal du Midi,

Private moorings on the banks of the Lez.

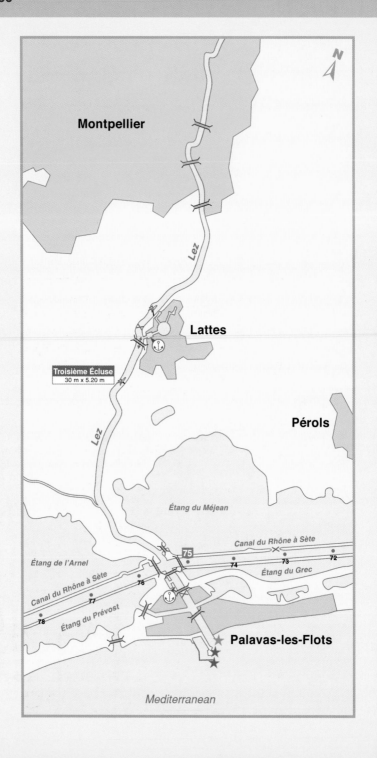

Montpellier

Lez

Lattes

Troisième Écluse
30 m x 5.20 m

Lez

Pérols

Étang du Méjean

Canal du Rhône à Sète

75

74 73 72

Étang de l'Arnel

Étang du Grec

Canal du Rhône à Sète

76

77

78 *Étang du Prévost*

Palavas-les-Flots

Mediterranean

and lies directly next to a weir. Those who wish to pass through the lock telephone the harbour master's office at the marina at Lattes (Port de Plaisance Ariane) from the control hut by the lock. At the *Capitainerie* there are three screens giving a full view of the upper and lower reaches, above and below the lock as well as a view of the chamber. The sluices and gates are remotely operated from the *Capitainerie* or by someone attending from the marina. Before the lower gate, a pontoon has been provided to simplify mooring and for landing a crew member. A red light means that the lock is shut but can be opened if you call.

On the east bank, a kilometre upstream from the lock, a mighty flood gate can be seen which can be closed when the Lez is in spate. Behind it stand upmarket apartments, visible from afar, surrounding Port Ariane. The developers have attempted to give these waterside homes a flavour of Venice, giving Italian names to each of the apartment blocks grouped around the marina. Here, within sight of your own balcony,

Troisième lock is remotely operated from the Capitainerie at Lattes.

you can moor your boat and, whenever you fancy a trip to the coast, motor out into the river and cruise down the Lez to the Mediterranean. A hire-boat company has been established at Port Ariane, and during the week, when its boats are in use, there will be plenty of free berths in addition to the 12 allocated to visitors. Two restaurants and a small supermarket are located here.

Further development of the canal and the building of more apartments, northwards towards Montpellier, have been planned for years, involving the refurbishment of a second lock and the creation of Port Marianna (another marina with apartment blocks) in the outskirts of Montpellier. The developers have obviously recognised the value of property with moorings right outside the front door, and boat owners and those who charter have these developers to thank for the reopening of the Lez river.

Port Ariane.

ÉTANG DE THAU

The Étang de Thau is a lagoon, roughly 17 kilometres long and 4 kilometres wide, which is connected to the Mediterranean at Sète and Marseillan and is therefore saline. It is renowned for its oyster and mussel beds which occupy almost half the surface area off the north-west shore.

In order to reach the Canal du Midi from the Canal du Rhône à Sète, you have to cross this stretch of open water. Over a large area, up to a mile off the seaward south-east shore, it is shallow. Here you can see the remains of the old canal bed where, for centuries, inland craft, with no engines and no sails (their masts had been lowered to clear the bridges) had to be pulled across the Étang de Thau.

Crossing the *étang* will be a new experience for some skippers and crews more used to gentle motoring along canals and rivers in craft designed for inland waterways. You

The beacon off Sète, marking the entrance to the Étang de Thau.

should take precautions before crossing the *étang* as the ride could be choppy; remember to safely stow that open wine carafe and vase of flowers and any other items that could slide off the saloon table on to the floor.

The authorities warn against crossing the lagoon when the wind is greater than force 4, when the waves on the open shallow water will have foaming crests. These short waves are unpleasant rather than dangerous. The real danger is that boats with tall superstructures and under-powered engines will not be able to maintain their course in strong winds and can be blown onto the oyster beds or more seriously towards the shallows off the south-east side of the *étang*.

There are also warnings that the cost of having to call out any of the rescue services, payable by the skipper in distress, can be considerable. When the mistral blows in stormy gusts from the hills, you should not even think about leaving your moorings. The wind is generally lower in the mornings and evenings. The warning notices contain a telephone number that you can ring for advice on whether or not the conditions are suitable for the crossing.

As you head west to cross the Étang de Thau from the Canal du Rhône à Sète, you will see the red and black striped light tower of Roquérols which is built on a stone foundation. On the Sète side, a black and yellow daymark warns you of the shallows along the south-east side of the lagoon. Passing between the two, a compass bearing of 227° from the light-house of Roquérols takes you to the entrance into the Canal du Midi which is marked by Les Onglous lighthouse; coming in the opposite direction, the bearing is 47°. At a speed of 10 kilometres per hour, that means a crossing of about an hour and a half.

Even if visibility is good, the light structures either end of the *étang* may not be in sight for the whole passage, but Mont St Loup near Agde, and coming in the opposite direction, Mont St Clair near Sète will be visible. Motoring towards the Canal

237

238

239

Étang du
Bagnas

Canal du Midi

240

Marseillan-
Plage

Les
Onglous

Marseillan

Oyster
beds

Oyster
beds

Mediterranean

Étang de Thau

Mèze

la Corniche

Mont
Saint-
Claire

Oyster
beds

Sète

Balaruc-
les-Bains

Bouzigues

Bassin des
Eaux Blanches

97

Canal de
la Peyrade
(not navigable)

Canal du Rhône à Sète

Balaruc-
le-Vieux

96

du Midi you should keep the landward foot of the hill as the point to home in on; in the opposite direction the foot of Sète's own little hill on the Étang de Thau side indicates the approximate direction. Those who have no compass on board will be safer if they take the suggested route for inland craft, keeping just outside the oyster beds. It is true that it is somewhat longer, but you are more likely to avoid the danger of being driven into the shallows off the south-east shore.

On this route, you steer west from the Roquérols light tower to pass just outside the oyster beds, which are unmistakable, extending 2 kilometres off the shoreline. If you decide to chug around among the oyster beds or even tie up to them, you will get about as much sympathy from the fishermen as somebody who lights a barbecue in a vineyard.

The church towers of Mèze and Marseillan are further landmarks. Wide, funnel-shaped entrances lead you to the harbours there. The route in open water past the entrance to

Pleasure boats have now taken over the old harbour at Mèze.

Masts of the many pleasure boats identify
Marseillan.

Mèze towards Les Onglous leads in a south-westerly direction, once again past extensive oyster beds. At the entrance to the Canal du Midi, the Glenans sailing school has established a base. The many masts belonging to the sailing boats seen near the lighthouse, confirm you are heading for the Canal du Midi entrance.

Visits to the harbours of Mèze and Marseillan are possible, and for a modest fee you can spend the night here. The quayside mooring places for visiting boats in both places are to starboard on entering the harbours. Water and fuel are available. Each harbour has a small marina for local boats. The one in Marseillan is directly next to the old harbour. The harbour master in the *Capitainerie* overlooking the entrance is responsible for berths in the marina and in the old harbour.

In Mèze, the oyster fishermen have been moved out eastwards to their own basin. The old harbour has been taken over by sailing boats; visitors can moor immediately

Marseillan harbour.

after the entrance, directly behind the mole next to the harbour master's office where, however, they are exposed to the wind and sometimes to the waves.

Whilst Mèze encourages visitors, Marseillan has retained the unspoilt atmosphere of an old fishing port. There are a number of restaurants around the harbour, but the short walk into the centre is worth the effort. For those who decide to dine ashore, try Table d'Emilie, for an upmarket menu at affordable prices. Alternatively, you can dine outside at Jardin de Naris.

For the more adventurous, who are confident about manoeuvring their boat in a confined space, opposite Sète on the Étang de Thau lies Bouzigues, the smallest fishing village on the lagoon. Here everything is just a little more relaxed. The small harbour has been extended by the addition of a wooden walkway behind piled-up rocks. Here, too, the fishing boats have been moved out to their own basin on the east side of the harbour.

For those who have so far resisted the temptation to dive into the murky waters of canals and rivers, it is worth mentioning that the water in the Étang de Thau is clear. The bottom can be seen even when the water is several metres deep. The sun soon warms up the water to bathing temperature. Hire-boats are equipped with anchors so that swimmers can plunge into the water in the middle of the lagoon, but do not be one of those skippers who fails to check whether the anchor chain is secured to the boat, and loses both anchor and chain on the bed of the *étang*.

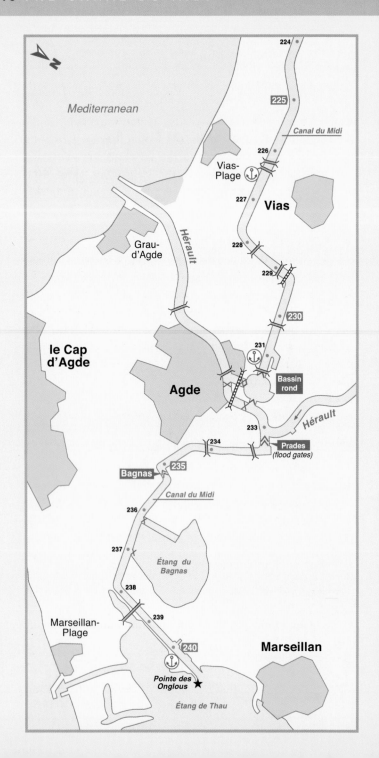

CANAL DU MIDI

The Canal du Midi begins quite inconspicuously with the mole on which Les Onglous lighthouse stands. Beyond the mole is a quay where sailing boats are moored. If approaching the Étang de Thau from the west, there will usually be space to moor up here to prepare the boat for crossing the open waters of the *étang*. The mole, exposed to the elements, can be an unsuitable place for a night stopover, and the quay beyond the sailing boats is reserved for commercial shipping.

Ahead, as far as the first lock, both sides of the canal have collapsed, and there is little sign of any towpath. After the first bridge, the Midi curves round to the right. Mooring here for the night is not recommended as the busy railway line from Marseille to Toulouse, which branches off to Spain at Narbonne, runs right next to the canal. The first five kilometres of the Midi are not very appealing, especially the nearer you get to the first lock at Bagnas. The explanation is that salt water from the Étang de Thau is washed into the brackish canal which runs close by the freshwater lake of Bagnas. Fish from the lake find their way into the saline

Les Onglous lighthouse marks the end of the Étang de Thau and the start of the Canal du Midi.

canal and die there. Not even the carrion-eating seagulls can effectively clean up this section of the canal.

Above the lock, which acts as a barrier to the salt water, the canal is clear. The Écluse de Bagnas is the first of the distinctive Midi oval lock chambers, originally 30 metres long, which were lengthened by 10 metres in the 1980s. Keeping the oval shape was sensible not only for aesthetic reasons, but from a practical point of view: the distinctive shape can accommodate two 3.50-metre wide hire-boats alongside each other. This made it possible to handle four or five 12 – 15 metre charter boats at any one time.

During the last few years all locks have been electrified, so keep-fit enthusiasts who anticipate building up their strength by manually turning the handle to work the sluices all the way along the route to Toulouse will be disappointed.

Three kilometres past the Bagnas lock is the entrance into the River Hérault. Two obstacles have to be navigated before the

The modest start of the Canal du Midi waterway.

river. First, there is a sharp bend to the left just beyond the road bridge. *Péniche* skippers, with their steering positions in the stern are driving 30 metres and more of boat-length blindly before them into the bends. They have no choice but to feel their way round the bend at slow ahead, sounding the horn as they approach and turn. Pleasure boat skippers should listen for an approaching vessel and, if all clear, hug the right hand bank to round the corner. If there is any sight or sound of a vessel approaching, wait until all is clear before proceeding.

Shortly after this bend comes the Prades flood lock. At normal water level, these gates stay open. If, after heavy rain, the Hérault rises only 20 centimetres, then this *écluse de garde* comes into operation to protect the Midi from flooding. Because it is of more recent construction, it is built with parallel lock walls. Midi traffic then uses a short one-kilometre section of the Hérault river between the flood lock and the famous round lock at Agde. Instead of heading downriver for one kilometre, a boat can motor up the Hérault for 5 kilometres as far as Bessan.

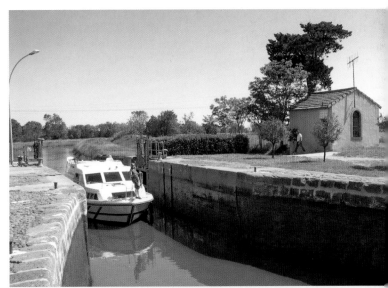

Entering the characteristic Midi oval lock
at Bagnas.

The flood lock at Prades is generally open.

The Hérault gives its name to the *Département* and to the local wine. The one-kilometre stretch of river between Prades *écluse de garde* and Agde's *bassin rond* is particularly wide, with a modest current tamed by a weir downstream of Agde's railway bridge that spans the river. On this one-kilometre stretch, there is the opportunity to hand over the steering for a few minutes to beginners and children as the river is so wide that any zig-zagging will be of little consequence.

AGDE

The entrance channel to the round lock at Agde seems all the narrower after the wide river. Agde's lock is a curiosity. Originally it was circular with a diameter of 30 metres. Through its three sets of gates, boats were able to, and today still can, travel towards Béziers, towards Agde and the Mediterranean, and also towards the Étang de Thau. In the process of upgrading the lock, only a quarter of the basin was enlarged. Vessels coming from Sète and heading for Agde can turn 90° to port in the lock without problems, even if they are longer than 30 metres. Heading straight ahead towards Béziers, vessels up to 40 metres long have no problems either. Only a barge longer than 30 metres coming from Béziers and wanting to turn to starboard, to gain access to Agde and the maritime Hérault, has difficulties. The sensible thing to do is to go straight across the lock in the direction of the Étang de Thau and through the gates into the broad waters of the Hérault, where the vessel can turn and head back into the lock to make the easier turn to port. Although traffic through the lock is not exactly hectic, the *basin rond* is controlled by lights. Normally the lock keeper will wait until at least a couple of pleasure boats are waiting before switching to green. This cannot be to preserve water as there will be water in abundance in the Hérault and a rise/fall of no more than half a metre in the basin.

The lock keeper pays particular attention to preventing any unauthorised passage through the third set of gates into the Hérault. The free berths alongside Agde's fishing boat quays may look tempting, but all hire-boats are prohibited from using this maritime section of the Hérault river, which

A typical Canal du Midi scene with plane trees lining both banks.

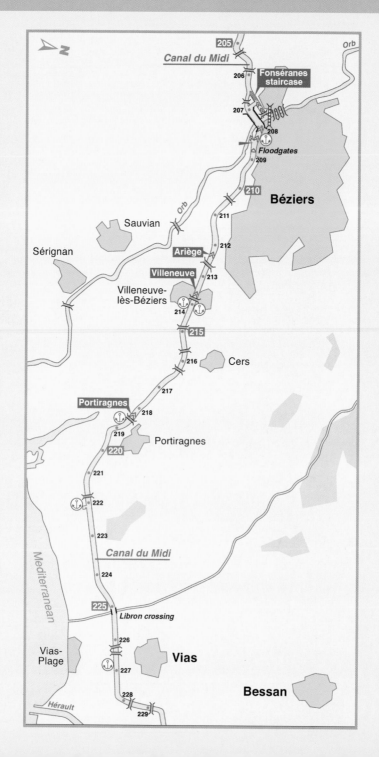

The bassin rond at Agde.

extends from Agde to the sea at le Grau-d'Agde. For Midi canal users, a marina has been dug out on the Béziers side of the round lock, accommodating a variety of private boats in various states of repair and a hire-boat base. It is not a particularly inviting spot, but it is worth mooring up here or alongside the canal bank either before or after the round lock to visit the one-time Greek colonised town of Agde. The approaches to the town from the moorings are not exactly encouraging, involving a route-march across the busy road bridge over the canal and then along a pedestrian walkway under the railway and across another road bridge spanning the maritime Hérault.

Agde is dominated by a cathedral, originally built as a fortified church. The narrow alleyways tempt you to enjoy a stroll in the shade. Agde is today 5 kilometres inland, but it is still packed with fishing boats landing the day's catch and providing an interesting view for diners in the many fish restaurants lining the quay.

CROSSING THE RIVER LIBRON

After the round lock at Agde there is a 13-kilometre lock-free pound lined with reed banks, plane trees and cypresses. After 6 kilometres, the canal then passes through a strange construction made up of chambers and gates, sluices, chains, trolleys, levers and windlasses, the purpose of which is hard to comprehend. This puzzling structure is built where the Canal du Midi crosses the River Libron. Normally a few feet lower than the Midi, the river flows gently through a culvert beneath the canal. The *Oeuvre du Libron* is a unique piece of engineering to cope with the rare occasions that the river is in flood when the culvert can no longer handle the deluge of water. The engineers built two huge flood chambers, which operate like lock gates, with the river's flood water flowing through first one chamber and then the other. This allows the river to cross the canal several feet higher than the Midi, at considerable strength, without causing so much as a ripple on the Midi and allowing canal traffic unimpeded and uninterrupted navigation during serious flood conditions.

Crossing the River Libron: the river flows under the canal.

Compare this with a similar situation on the Canal du Rhône à Sète where there are flood gates positioned where the River Vidourle crosses the canal. When the river is in flood, the gates are closed to protect the canal, and shipping is stopped until the water level drops and the flood gates can be re-opened.

There is a *Le Boat* base 2.5 kilometres farther on at Port Cassafières on the south bank. If you only need to fill up with water and diesel, you need not berth in the port. Right on the canal there is a landing stage suitable for a short stop. This base boasts a restaurant, useful for those who want a rest from galley cooking. The hire-boat bases are engaged in tough but friendly competition with one another. Those that help out a stranger with his boat (serious technical problems tend to be made more difficult by the many different kinds of engines) do so in the hope of gaining a new customer on the crew's next trip.

If you are planning to cycle or walk down to the sea (only a kilometre and a half from the canal) you have to stop at the Vias road bridges which is east of the Libron crossing, or the road bridge just west of Port Cassafières. The local authority at Vias have provided a decent little jetty with a telephone box and fresh water supply.

PORTIRAGNES

Portiragnes is where the 13-kilometre long canal pound without locks ends. From here to Béziers, beside the canal, a cycle track with tarmac surface has been laid down. The towpath is reserved for pedestrians. The existence of this track makes it very appealing for one of the crew to cycle between locks, at the most four and a half kilometres apart. Between Villeneuve and Ariège, the A9 motorway crosses over the canal. Officially, tying up on this section is forbidden, but in reality who would really like to have their lunch break or their night's rest disturbed by the high noise-level of a motorway.

From Portiragnes onwards, the banks are lined by tall plane trees. Older, narrow bridges alternate with newer, wide-span ones. The older ones make better photographic subjects but demand more care when passing beneath them. The National Trunk Road 112 runs right alongside the canal on the outskirts of Béziers. As long as the boat is under power, the sound of the diesel engine drowns out the traffic noise, but this canal section is not a good place to spend the night, especially as the busy railway from Montpellier to Narbonne joins the stream of traffic approaching the town.

At the fourth bridge after the Ariège lock, you come upon a flood gate which is used to prevent floodwater from the Orb River pouring into the canal. Up until the middle of the 19th century, the Canal du Midi included a short section of the Orb in the navigation. To-day this part of the river serves only to feed the Canal du Midi with water. Shortly before the lock at Béziers, the Canalet du Pont Rouge (Little Canal of the Red Bridge) branches off to the left. You can turn into this disused backwater and moor up in a quiet spot.

On this stretch of canal, two hire-boats have room to pass comfortably.

BÉZIERS

At one time, boatmen used to travel upstream on the Orb and then, shortly before where the railway bridge is today, turn off left into what is nowadays a disused section of canal. This is where the harbour of Béziers, with the name of Port Notre Dame, was situated. Because the floodwaters on the Orb always brought commercial shipping to a halt, in 1857 a canal bridge over the river was opened. Built in the neo-classical style of those times, it is one of the attractions of the canal. From the bridge is a wonderful view over Béziers, the town on the hill, and over the other bridges across the Orb – four altogether, new and old. But before you reach the Orb aqueduct, you still have two locks to negotiate and the present-day harbour of Béziers to cross. These locks also date from the middle of the 1800s and they do not have Riquet's oval-shaped chambers. Originally, before and after the harbour, was a double and triple staircase lock. In the process of modernisation, the locks were not only electrified, fitted with illuminated signs and lengthened to 40.5 metres, they also joined the several chambers together, so that now

The quiet backwater of Canalet du Pont Rouge before Béziers lock provides a peaceful mooring.

The famous aqueduct over the Orb at Béziers.

The view of the old town of Beziers from above the canal.

the lift in Béziers lock is 4.24 metres and 6.19 metres in Orb lock. Entering such deep chambers when climbing the Midi can be a little intimidating, and the crew may wonder if their lines are going to be long enough to reach the top of the chamber until they discover the vertical poles set into the lock walls. The lines are simply passed around the poles and slide up or down as the boat rises or drops.

In the past, at the harbour in Béziers, there was refuelling alongside. Today if you need to top up with fuel, you can do it *en route* at many of the hire-boat bases; a small operator is located in Béziers.

The various hire-boat companies make a fuel charge, which covers fuel, oil and gas, based on engine running hours. (*Le Boat* charged 3.5 euros per hour in 2009 for their smallest craft). Normally a full tank of fuel would be sufficient for a

week's hire. If a boat is chartered for longer, tokens are used to pay at any of the charter company bases. If the charterer has to pay cash elsewhere, they are reimbursed by deducting the euros paid from the final total based on the engine running hours. Not all the hire-boat bases have fuel pumps that have been calibrated to supply diesel to the public.

The harbour at Béziers has been refurbished in recent years. They have built up the quays, landscaped the banks and among the older warehouses there are now offices and apartment blocks. Plane trees provide some shade on the quay where you can moor. From here, you can take a short stroll to the river where the aqueduct makes a more impressive sight from the land compared with the view from the boat as you motor over the Orb. Although the Canal du Midi lies to the south of the town centre, Béziers is worth a visit. The main promenade is Allées Paul Riquet, named after the Canal du Midi's creator who was born here. A larger than life-size statue, dating from the year 1838, dominates the plane tree-lined boulevard with a central reservation forming a pedestrian way and a site for street traders. Béziers, with a population of approximately 70,000, is the largest town along the route of the Canal du Midi, apart from Toulouse, which is its final destination.

The now peaceful town of Beziers had a violent history. In 1209, in a bloody crusade against the Cathars, directed by the Papal Legate Arnaud Amaury, it is estimated that 20,000 people were massacred – some even killed in churches as they sought sanctuary.

To the south, at the end of Allées Paul Riquet, the old town extends up the hill. At St Nazaire Cathedral, the observation platform at the top provides a wonderful view over the Orb valley and the plain crossed by the Canal du Midi. At the lower end of Allées Paul Riquet is the Plateau des Poètes, a park near the railway station and the harbour. In summer, the beautifully landscaped park is the venue for a festival in the open-air theatre.

THE STAIRCASE LOCKS AT FONSÉRANES

In order to get to see one of Béziers' main sights, you do not even need to leave the boat: the Canal du Midi leads from the aqueduct over the Orb through a short cypress-lined stretch of canal to the staircase locks at Fonséranes. Built right next to a former health spa which is now a retirement home, the 9-chambered staircase of locks achieved a climb or drop of 24 metres, measuring from the Orb's water level. When the aqueduct was built over the Orb, the number of chambers making up the staircase was reduced to six to achieve a reduced lift/drop of 13.60 metres. The locks are electrified. In season, the operating hours for climbing are from 10.00 until 12.15 and from 16.00 until 18.45; the descending traffic time-table is from 08.00 to 09.30 and 13.00 to 15.30. Commercial shipping has priority. Alongside the Fonséranes staircase of locks is a remarkable *pente d'eau* (water slope) which was in operation for 20 years. This type of boat lift was developed during the period of general improvements to the canal when it was realised that it would be impractical to lengthen the chambers of Fonséranes

The arrow points the way to the Fonséranes staircase locks, avoiding the closed water slope.

staircase to accommodate larger vessels. The lift worked on the same principle as the one still operating at Montech beside the Garonne canal, hauling water and craft up and down a 272-metre long concrete trench. With the decline in barge traffic on the Midi, Fonséranes' water slope was finally abandoned in the 1990s, but is still retained as a piece of waterway engineering history.

Above Fonséranes' staircase is yet another of Paul Riquet's strokes of genius – by ingenious planning, he created a 53-kilometre stretch of canal without a single lock, and achieved this not across a broad plain but along the edge of hilly countryside. He followed a contour line by creating a waterway with numerous sharp bends, necessitating the canal traffic having to execute some extremely tight turns. In this section, before such bends, it is very important to keep to the right. Tooting the horn may help, even if the rather feeble horns on pleasure boats can barely be heard. These bends, by the way, were a source of exasperation to the planners involved in upgrading the canal, because they

The disused water slope at Fonséranes.

realised that it is simply not enough to just lengthen the lock chambers. Barges of the standard measurement of 38.5 metres would have great difficulty in getting round the bends, not to mention the hazard of inexperienced amateurs coming the other way. So that barges could carry a full 350-tonne load in place of the 150 tonnes they can take today, the planners realised the canal would have to be dredged another 40 centimetres. The alternative would be to raise the water level but that would be prohibitively uneconomical with bridges, lock gates and chambers all having to be correspondingly raised, embankments strengthened and the towpath, so useful for breakdown services, heightened. With the decline in barge traffic, this project to deepen the Midi has long since been abandoned. The canal route is unchanged, dug out over 300 years ago, and still bearing witness to the genius who was its builder.

In Colombiers, six kilometres from Béziers, the hire-boat company Locaboat has established a marina. With its old wash house next to the bridge, Colombiers is typical of the

Fonséranes staircase in the early morning.

The hotel barges are now the largest craft to be seen on the Midi.

unspoilt villages strung out along the canal from here onwards. Around the marina, a lively commercial area has sprung up, with a chemist, a newspaper shop and a café. The nearby château houses a restaurant with an attractive terrace. Eating out anywhere near the canal will always be a gamble – some family innkeepers make a big effort to please even short-stay guests with regional cooking. However, there are also the bandits of the culinary scene who make their money by selling unpalatable fast food. After all, they are not dependant on repeat custom from the crews of passing boats, and can foist their poor menus on unsuspecting tourists that they will never see again. With seven to eight thousand craft passing the door every year, they will still make a good living. Fortunately, all boats also have a galley on board.

THE MALPAS TUNNEL

A kilometre and a half past Colombiers, the tunnel at Malpas comes into sight; at 161 metres long, 6 metres wide and with 5 metres of lofty headroom, you can look right through it from end to end. It can only take one-way traffic,

Malpas tunnel.

but there is no rule regarding who has priority, and no regulating traffic signals.

Before you enter the Malpas tunnel, you should consider taking a short walk to the Oppidum d'Ensérune. You can tie up on the north bank about a 100 metres before the tunnel entrance, then take a path to the road that climbs the hill for a kilometre to the excavated site of the *oppidum*. Occupied by the Iberians in 600BC, the walls can be seen and many valuable excavated artefacts are displayed in the museum which is open in the mornings. From the high ground of the *oppidum*, there is a remarkable view to the north of the Étang de Montady. This drained lagoon, surrounded by fields, which are neatly criss-crossed by irrigation channels, gives the multi-coloured landscape the appearance of a giant dart board.

If the attraction on the hill is evidence of pre-Roman times, the next village of Poilhes offers traces of a later occupation by the Romans. On the quay here, you can look into a pit claimed to have once been a Roman storeroom. Poilhes was

The Étang de Montady viewed from the *oppidum*.

one of the first villages on the canal, which with facilities for disposing of rubbish and replenishing water, attracts skippers to moor up here. They now charge for the moorings. Most local authorities have discovered that attracting visiting boats on the Midi helps the restaurants and local trade, and have cleaned up the quays and laid on a supply of fresh water for which they may charge – which tends to deter those who scrub the decks using drinking water when a bucketful from the canal would do the job.

CAPESTANG

Six kilometres farther on, still in the shade of the plane trees, you sight the Cathedral of Capestang, which dominates the village skyline. Above the tower, the red and yellow Occitan flag was a sign of regional independence until it was replaced by the *tricolour*.

The best place to moor is between the two bridges – one steel, which leads to the now closed railway station, and the old stone bridge with its dramatically low headroom.

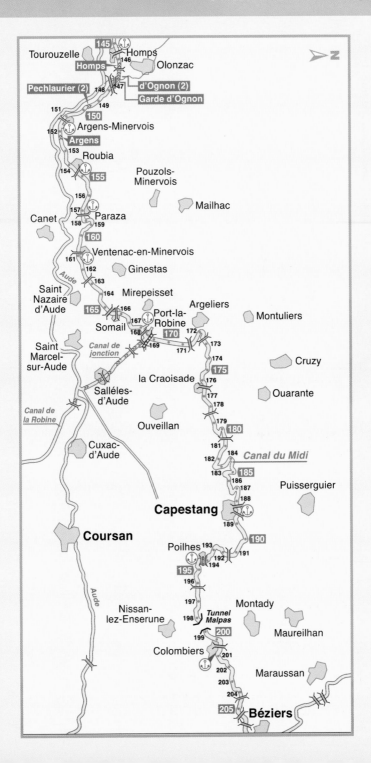

So many people now tie up here that there are often boats mooring on both sides and getting through the stone bridge can be tight, and delayed by oncoming traffic. Water and fuel are available here and it is only a short distance from the centre of the village. There is a market held here on Sunday mornings.

Beyond Capestang comes a winding stretch of canal with several hairpin bends where the skipper must pay particular attention. Plane trees line both sides of the canal, their roots serving to reinforce the banks to stop them from collapsing. The cool shade from the trees helps to reduce water loss and protects the crews of pleasure craft from the blazing sun. Comparing what nature has provided with the artificial strengthening of the banks of other canals, be they of stone, concrete or iron, these plane trees and their roots not only look much more beautiful, but are clearly a longer lasting solution.

The stretch between Capestang and Port-la-Robine is decidedly picturesque and solitary. For around 20 kilometres there is not

Capestang is a popular stop-over.

Approaching the low bridge at Capestang.

Roots of the plane trees reinforce the banks
between Capestang and Port-la-Robine.

even a waterside village, with the occasional farm the only sign of civilisation in the somewhat remote countryside.

The village closest to the canal is Argeliers, some four kilometres east of Port-la-Robine, on a 180° bend. The attractive old bridge, with a restaurant with cypress trees close by, look as though they belong in a painting. After just under a kilometre along the nearly deserted road, you are in the village with all the shopping facilities.

For a long time the villages on the Canal du Midi, with their peaceful ambience and reluctance to change seemed to belong to another era. Things have changed in recent years. Next to the village centres, groups of new homes have been built; the houses are rendered in the local earthy ochre colour, but *en masse* they all look rather uniform.

Where the Canal de Jonction/Canal de la Robine or *Embranchement de la Nouvelle* (see map on page 91) branch

It is single file traffic along the aqueduct over the River Cesse.

off in the direction of Narbonne and Port-la-Nouvelle, you are advised to proceed at reduced speed and keep a sharp lookout. Visibility is reduced because three bridges span the junction. Immediately after the furthest of the three bridges, on the right-hand side, is Port-la-Robine, a rather crowded, private marina with re-fuelling facilities. Right after the marina comes the aqueduct over the River Cesse, and, like most canal bridges over rivers, it is one-way traffic only. There is no overtaking between the busy junction and the end of the aqueduct (where there is a small restaurant) or vice-versa if east-going.

LE SOMAIL

Less than 2 kilometres beyond the Cesse aqueduct lies the little village of Le Somail. Its old hump-backed bridge and the buildings on both banks look as if they might have been classified as historical monuments. Postcards and posters of the Canal du Midi will invariably feature Le Somail which attracts

The period stone buildings of Le Somail are one of many attractions of the Canal du Midi.

visitors in great numbers by water and by road. The waterside restaurants, above and below the bridge, look very inviting, but in summer the overworked staff have to cope with coach-loads of diners. Crews from passing boats, wanting to dine ashore, may wish to move on to find a less crowded eating place.

LANGUEDOC, THE WINE-GROWING REGION

From here on, all the way to Carcassonne, the Canal du Midi runs along the valley of the River Aude, which you can sometimes catch glimpses of from the boat as you motor along. The river and canal roughly mark the boundary between two well-known wine-growing districts - Minervois to the north and Corbières to the south. Together they form the largest continuous vineyard in the world, stretching eastwards to Montpellier and beyond. Minervois and Corbières were in the headlines in the early 1970s, when the winegrowers were protesting against the policies of the central government in Paris. Age-old wounds were opened up. These dated back to the 13th century when there was violent repression of the Cathar religious movement and the Occitan language, which was a mixture of Italian, Catalonian and French, and from which the region derived its name – Languedoc or Language of Oc.

After some fatalities from the skirmishes between the winegrowers and the police in 1977, the demonstrations ceased. However, the problems of over-production of wine in this region have not been resolved. Here and there you see fallow land and fields that have been turned over to other produce, such as asparagus, tomatoes or sunflowers. The cultivation of olive groves seem to be worthwhile once again, as evidenced by newly laid-out plantations.

The countryside of the Minervois and Corbières districts is very beautiful so set yourself a leisurely pace to appreciate the scenery. As the district is hilly to mountainous, exploring by bicycle from the boat is only possible to a limited extent.

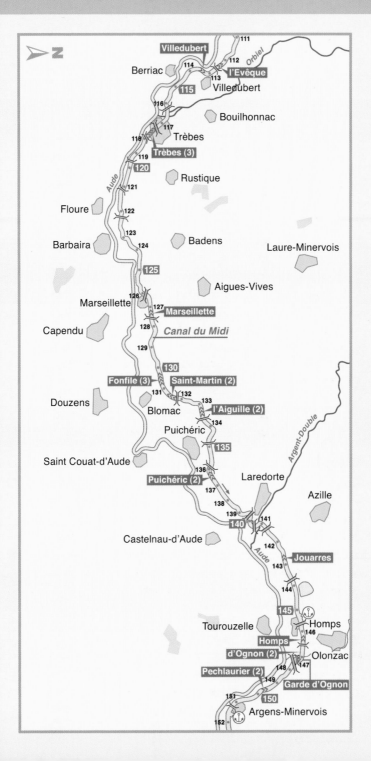

If you can find somewhere to stay for a couple of nights, either before or after the boat trip you will really be able to appreciate the countryside; accommodation in these parts will certainly be more affordable than at the seaside resorts.

The little town of Minerve, after which the entire district is named, is definitely worth seeing. It stands on a cliff protected on three sides. The Cathars built a fortress here which, in spite of its commanding position, was captured by the crusading Catholics. The River Cesse in these parts has, over the centuries, sculpted a canyon and, where it disappears underground, has hollowed out caves.

Another recommended trip is to the south to Lagrasse. This small town enjoys a relatively peaceful existence during the week, cut off from the world and protected by the hills all around. You can reach it from Carcassonne or from Lézignan on winding roads. At the weekend in Lagrasse and in Minerve, expect to meet hoards of day-trippers from the surrounding area.

Lézignan, a centre for the Corbières wine trade (and the winegrowers' demonstrations) can be visited from the canal. From Argens-Minervois it is only six kilometres on the main road. The museum in Lézignan, devoted to winegrowing, is located in an old vineyard.

On the 50-kilometre stretch of Midi between Le Somail and Trèbes, there are no towns beside the canal, but many delightful, hospitable waterside villages, each one appearing to be an unspoilt little community. A visitor, stopping off at one of these villages, can watch a game of *boules* on the village square in the late afternoon or just relax with the locals in a bar. Here there may be surprises as, deep in this winegrowing region, you may discover that the landlord has a job to find you a bottle of wine. The explanation is that although the locals make their own wine, in the village bar they tend to drink pastis, coffee or beer.

The huge church-like waterside wine cellar in Ventenac.

In general, the Minervois and Corbière wines, with their delicate, subtle flavours, are light and pleasant to drink. Owing to overproduction, much of the local wine is used for blending and shipped off to Bordeaux where the harvests are smaller but the profits greater.

One of the attractions of mooring in Ventenac-en-Minervois, which is just 5 kilometres upstream of Le Somail, is a majestic building, which at first sight appears to be a church. Inside, however, any worshiping is directed towards the local Minervois wines, for the building is used as a huge waterside wine cellar open to the public. You can eat and drink in Ventenac in surroundings which are as unpretentious as they are affordable.

With the lock at Argens between Roubia and Argens-Minervois, comes the end of the 53-kilometre lockless pound. Argens-Minervois is one of the most beautiful of the

Cruising through Argens-Minervois.

A busy quayside at Homps.

Minervois villages, dominated on one side of the canal by the 14th century château and with the River Aude meandering along the other side. Locaboat have established a base in Port Occitanie, where there are many facilities for canal boats.

Approximately 3 kilometres above Argens-Minervois, without warning, you come upon a traffic light (usually green) on the bridge before a flood gate. Where are the floods supposed to come from? The keeper of the two-chambered nearby Ognon lock provides the answer. The seemingly insignificant little River Ognon which normally trickles underneath the canal can, in the event of cloudbursts in the hills, swell to such an extent that it floods the canal. The keeper here has experienced this several times when he has had to close the floodgate, preventing through navigation until the floods subside.

Almost everywhere along the canal, the locals have realised that there is good business to be made from passing boats. At the next village, Homps, they have developed not one but

This floodgate can be closed when River Ognon is in spate.

two harbours where Connoisseur (*Le Boat*) and Camargue Plaisance have established bases for their fleets of charter boats. Around each of these marinas there is a choice of restaurants offering anything from a simple pizza to menus with several courses, and there is always the option of sitting outside with a waterside view.

There are well over a hundred bridges crossing the Midi. The most original shapes are the aqueducts where you travel on water over water, the most impressive being the previously-mentioned Orb bridge at Béziers. Shortly before Laredorte, where the narrow hairpin bends once again make extra caution essential, on the bank an ancient-looking multi-arched structure comes into sight. This curious waste-weir or spillway, built by Vauban in 1693, regulates the water level. Just as important as the supply of water to the waterway is the need to prevent the canal from flooding after heavy rainfall. For this purpose, upstream of Jouarres lock, the excess water can be drained out of the canal over the side weir and through grills into a small side channel and fed back lower down into the canal. This

The spillway near Laradorte.

sometimes causes whirlpools and currents in front of the lower lock gates which did not worry the barges, but might be felt by a much lighter glassfibre pleasure boat during serious flooding.

The great majority of lock keepers along the Midi are friendly characters who have accepted that the maintenance of the canals – and their jobs – depends on the pleasure boat traffic. In the 1970s, things were different. *Éclusiers* thought that two or three barges a day were sufficient to justify their employment, and any pleasure boats were regarded more as a nuisance, distracting them from their gardening.

WINE TASTING AT THE LOCK

Even back in the 1970s, some of the lock keepers realised that the crews of passing pleasure boats represented a new outlet for selling fresh produce from the countryside. There was the enterprising keeper of the two-chambered Puichéric lock who sold wine from the cask that he kept in a shed next to the house. After sampling the wine, the crew of a passing craft would then wash out every possible container to take delivery by hose at minimal cost. With today's heavy pleasure-boat traffic on the Midi, there is no time in the locks for such an enterprise and one must generally rely on the village *alimentation* or *supermarché* for replenishments, although some business-minded lock keepers have stalls outside their houses with produce from their gardens and various home-made brews.

Of all the villages on the canal, Marseillette probably makes the bleakest impression; you motor past a cemetery and a large car park, where the local authority has installed a water supply. But in the village, overlooking the canal, as well as the ruins of a small castle, there is a hotel/restaurant with a terraced garden, a pizzeria and several shops.

TRÈBES

Near the three-chambered lock at Trèbes, a restaurant has been established in the old mill. Sitting in the shade of the large olive tree on its terrace, you have the panoramic view not only of the lock, but out over the Aude valley as far as the Montagne d'Alaric, reminding us that the Visigoths possessed a kingdom in these parts around the year 500AD.

Between the lock and the bridge is the busy town centre with good opportunities for shopping and a harbour where Connoisseur Cruisers (*Le Boat*) have established a base. There are more public moorings on the south bank opposite the cruiser hire base and beyond the bridge on the north side.

Shortly after leaving Trèbes, you cross a finely-restored aqueduct, built by Vauban in 1686, over the River Orbiel. After a further 8 kilometres, there is another aqueduct which carries both the canal and the road over the Fresquel river. The aqueduct is just beyond a curious arrangement of a single and double lock. In former times, the passengers on the canal's mail boat transferred here to waiting horse-drawn coaches and vice-versa. The locks at Fresquel are separated

The three-chambered lock at Trèbes.

Single and double locks at Fresquel.

with a 250-metre long pound between the lower and the two upper locks. One theory for this arrangement is that the River Fresquel feeds into the more substantial Aude River a short distance from the locks and there was a plan, never adopted, to use the Fresquel river to link the Midi with the Aude at this point – hence the pound between locks 42 and 43 for barges to turn to enter the proposed link.

CARCASSONNE

On the way to Carcassonne, the canal banks are lined with cypresses that replace the familiar plane trees which are much in evidence elsewhere along the canal in these parts. Towards Toulouse, there is a greater variety of trees: poplars, oaks, robinias, rowans and wild cherry feature amongst the plane trees and, in places, often replacing them completely. At the Villedubert lock between Trèbes and Carcassonne, palm trees remind us that we are on the Canal du Midi or the Canal of the South. The landscape along the canal has evidently changed over the centuries. A 1772 document notes a preponderance of poplars and willows sharing the canal banks with mulberry, elm, ash, fruit and olive trees.

The majority of the visitors to Carcassonne do not come by water, nor do they come by train. Carcassonne's railway station, canal harbour and lock lie beside each other, evidence of a history of transport systems continuing for more than 150 and 300 years respectively. Now a motorway passes to the south, on the far side of the town. This is the main access for the masses of visitors who come to view *la Cité*, the fortified old town. In the 19th century, it was restored to its original appearance as a medieval fortified town, which has since been used several times as a film set.

The majority of tourists wander around *la Cité*, along the cobbled alleyways lined with souvenir shops and cafés. Directly beside the Basilica of St Nazaire, which is half Gothic, half Romanesque, there is a semi-circular open-air arena. In July, Carcassonne tries to lure tourists away from

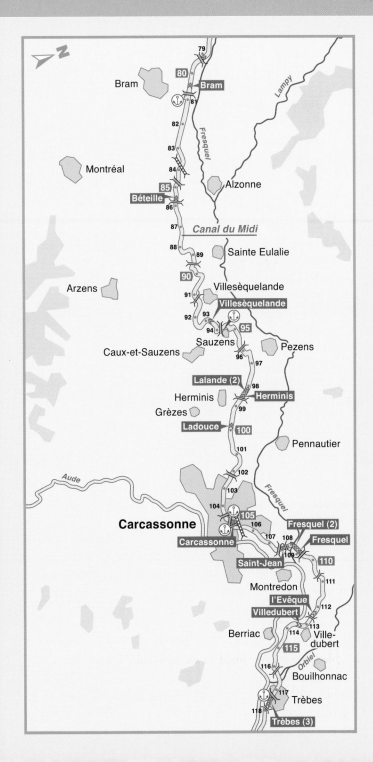

Bram

79

80

Bram

81

82

Fresquel

83

84

85

Béteille

86

Montréal

Alzonne

87

Canal du Midi

88

89

Sainte Eulalie

90

Arzens

Villesèquelande

91

Villesèquelande

92

93

94

95

Sauzens

96

97

Pezens

Caux-et-Sauzens

Lalande (2)

98

Herminis

Herminis

99

Grèzes

Ladouce

100

Pennautier

101

Aude

102

103

Fresquel

104

105

Carcassonne

106

Fresquel (2)

Carcassonne

107

108

Fresquel

109

Saint-Jean

110

111

Montredon

l'Evêque

112

Villedubert

113

Berriac

114

Ville-
dubert

115

116

Orbiel

Bouilhonnac

117

Trèbes

118

Trèbes (3)

La Cité, the medieval fortified town of Carcassonne.

the coast with a festival offering a mixture of attractions from Hamlet to music from Johnny Hallyday.

The lower part of town or *Ville Basse,* connected by two bridges over the River Aude, is not without historical significance. The hexagonal ground plan dates from the 13th century, evidenced by the narrowness of the streets which today function as one-way routes or pedestrian ways like rue Clémenceau, which is lined with shops of every kind, and extends all the way from the bridge by the lock to the town centre. There is no lack of historical architecture to take in, including a curious building with the façade of a 13th century Carmelite chapel but when you think you are entering a place of worship, you discover much of the interior now functions as a shopping centre.

Between Carcassonne and Castelnaudary, there is not much sign of habitation for 40 kilometres. Shopping can be a challenge, and there are fewer waterside bars and restaurants. There are, however, wonderful, quite unexpected surprises like the hamlet of Sauzens, about 10 kilometres after leaving Carcassonne, right in the middle of a slalom of narrow bends where they have built a jetty for visiting boats.

BRAM

Another mooring place worth a visit is Bram. By the bridge here is an old house belonging to the canal authority. The quay in front of the house is built with the same curvature as the Midi's distinctive lock chambers which suggests it dates back to the same period. Nowadays boats from a hire-boat company moor up here. Their office is in a lovely house with a picturesque terrace right on the canal bank – unfortunately a tourist trap selling overpriced ice cream and other refreshments. The centre of Bram is about a kilometre and a half along a road where cars race by, and there is neither a pavement nor a cycle track for the walker. The train on the Toulouse – Narbonne line stops in the town – a useful place to change crews. The main attraction of Bram is its centre which is built in a circular plan, particularly well-defined in aerial photographs.

Those who are not yet familiar with the locking routine will certainly be thoroughly experienced after another 16 kilometres of canal as far as Castelnaudary, with no less than 18 lock chambers, in various combinations, to climb 46 metres, finishing with the four-chambered staircase at St Roch, lifting boats into Castelnaudary's Grand Bassin.

After Tréboul lock, uninterrupted views of the countryside to the north open up because there are no longer trees lining the canal. The next lock bears the remarkable name of *Écluse de la Criminelle*. The name has no reflection on the above average lift in the lock (3.11 metres) but there is a local legend telling of mysterious happenings here – on one occasion, shying horses pulling a boat are reputed to have plunged into the pound. A former lock keeper here was an ardent supporter of Occitania and of the canal's constructor Pierre-Paul Riquet. He even painted the cross of the Count

Occitan symbols are displayed on the lock gates of the Ecluse de la Criminelle and the tricolour can be seen flying on the keeper's house.

The lock at Tréboul.

of Toulouse, the symbol of resistance against the North, on his lock gates.

CASTELNAUDARY

Entering the Grand Bassin at Castelnaudary, you have a wonderful view of the silhouette of the town as it appears to rise before you. It was even more imposing in earlier eras, as can be seen from views on old postcards when the skyline was filled with windmills. On the south bank is located the base belonging to Crown Blue Line, the British company which, as Blue Line, started the boat-hire business on the Canal du Midi at the beginning of the 1970s. As previously mentioned they now operate under the name *Le Boat*, with a large boatyard at Castelnaudary. Next to a newly-built, roofed repair dock is a traditional dry dock that you can visit. Opposite, on the north side, is a garage serving fuel to both cars and boats.

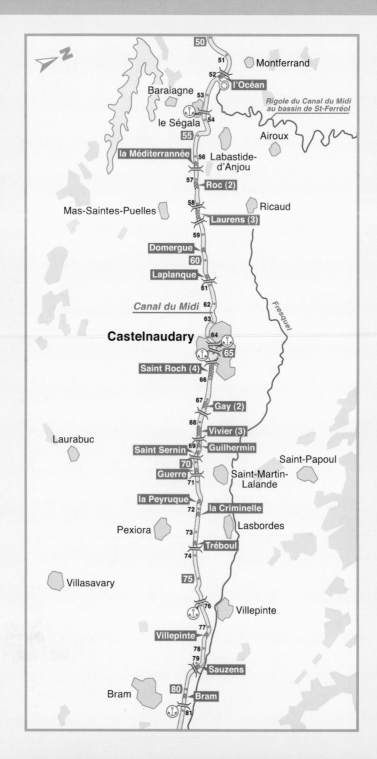

50

51 Montferrand

52 l'Océan

Baraiagne 53

Rigole du Canal du Midi au bassin de St-Ferréol

le Ségala 54

Airoux

55

la Méditerrannée 56 Labastide-d'Anjou

57 Roc (2)

58 Ricaud

Mas-Saintes-Puelles Laurens (3)

59

Domergue 60

Laplanque 61

Canal du Midi 62

63 Fresquel

Castelnaudary 64

65

Saint Roch (4) 66

67 Gay (2)

68 Vivier (3)

Saint Sernin 69 Guilhermin

Laurabuc 70

Guerre 71 Saint-Martin-Lalande

Saint-Papoul

la Peyruque 72 la Criminelle

73 Lasbordes

Pexiora Tréboul 74

75 Villasavary

76 Villepinte

77

Villepinte 78

79 Sauzens

80 Bram

Bram 81

Grand Bassin, Castelnaudary.

The water quality of Castelnaudary's Grand Bassin is demonstrated by the large numbers of fish that you can attract at dusk with a handful of breadcrumbs. In the afternoons, the local sailing school teaches the next generation the skills of dinghy sailing. The island in the Grand Bassin, with its high trees, was built in 1754 to reduce the effects of the strong westerly winds across the open water.

Castelnaudary, with its 11,000 population, claims to be the Cassoulet Capital. Cassoulet is a substantial stew containing haricot beans, mutton, sausage and goose dripping – in other words a real lock keeper's meal dating from the times when the gate paddles were cranked by hand. Those who enjoy the dish can take it home as a souvenir in tins available from the Hotel Fourcade in Place de la Liberté, where the chef has modestly christened his bean dish *l'Incomparable*.

West of Castelnaudary, boat traffic is noticeably reduced. This is because *Le Boat*'s base here tends to be the end of the route for those who charter on the Midi or the starting point for charterers heading south towards the Mediterranean. Other boat-hire companies recommend Castelnaudary to their customers as a cruise turning point.

In season, the Canal du Midi between the Étang de Thau and Castelnaudary is busy, and some would say overcrowded. This is particularly noticeable around and in the locks, where boats are grouped in fours and fives to go through together; often there will be another group up ahead, not to mention the oncoming traffic. But on the water 'more haste, less speed' applies, and those who feel the pace on the waterways is too slow should exchange their boat for a motorbike.

Of course, this system of passing through the locks in groups dictates the pace, and those who prefer to dawdle may be embarrassed by the critical exchanges between those who have to wait for them at every lock. The lock keepers let each other know by phone exactly how many boats are on the way, and if four have been reported at the last lock, the keeper will wait until all four are assembled at the next. These problems barely exist west of Castelnaudary – there you may be the only boat on the water for long stretches. It is good practice to inform the lock keeper that you intend to stop for a lunch break and to continue again at, say, 15.00; if you do this he will probably have the next lock standing open for you, unless there is an oncoming vessel already in the lock.

Fourteen kilometres above Castelnaudary, you reach the pass at Naurouze at a height above sea level of 190 metres. The 5-kilometre long pound is enclosed by the Écluse de la Méditerranée at one end and the Écluse de l'Océan at the other end. In the middle, at the little village of Le Ségala, a hire-boat base has been established. This is where the Canal du Midi reaches its highest point and, close to the Écluse de l'Océan, it is fed with water from the Montagne Noir (the Black Mountain). This water supply to the canal, from the reservoir of St Ferréol near the small town of Rével, was the canal's constructor Pierre-Paul Riquet's brilliant achievement. The reservoir was, in its day, the largest in the world. All previous plans had failed because no-one could figure out how to feed the higher sections of the canal in sufficient quantities of water, particularly during the dry summer months.

Riquet, whose forebears from Florence were originally called Arrigheti, later Riquetti, wanted to erect, at the Naurouze Pass, a statue of Louis XIV who had commissioned him to develop the project. The Canal du Midi for many years was called 'Canal Royal du Languedoc' (Royal Languedoc Canal) or 'Canal des Deux Mers' (Canal of the Two Seas). Instead of a statue of the 'Sun King', an obelisk was erected in 1827 overlooking the canal, which celebrates the brilliance and the tragedy of the Canal du Midi's creator. Pierre-Paul Riquet died at the age of 76, sadly only about six months before the canal was officially opened on 15 May

Beyond Méditerranée lock is La Ségala where the Canal du Midi reaches its highest point.

1681. He devoted the last 15 years of his life to planning, constructing and financing the canal. He left his heirs huge debts but also the right to operate the canal and to levy charges. But the debts were repaid many times over, because until its nationalisation at the end of the 18th century, Riquet's descendants enjoyed a good income due to the constantly increasing traffic on the Canal du Midi.

Immediately above Océan lock, you will find a quiet, atmospheric berth beneath ancient trees. From your mooring you can take a stroll to look at the engineering system used for supplying the canal with water, and it is only a few hundred metres to the obelisk where you can pay homage to the man who made your waterway cruise possible, and to the 12,000 men and women who worked on the Midi from 1667 until 1681.

The descent starts at Océan lock for Atlantic-bound craft.

PORT LAURAGAIS

Within a kilometre, a more modern kind of memorial has been established. At Port Lauragais, the moorings are combined with a motorway services area where the modern *Autoroute des Deux Mers* crosses over the canal. In addition to the *halte nautique* and a shop, there is a museum here dedicated to the Canal du Midi where you can discover, for example, that a horse can pull a 60-ton barge and that traffic on the Midi reached its peak in 1856, transporting 110 million tonnes of freight and 100,000 passengers (three times the number of modern pleasure boat users). In the second half of the 19th century, there was competition from the railways, but it was still nearly another 150 years before the last barge captain made the final journey along the Midi. Near the museum pavilion is an hotel, a restaurant, a souvenir shop and an architecturally interesting building which houses a Rugby Museum. This sport is very popular in the area of Toulouse.

Once past Castelnaudary, the vineyards slowly give way to broad fields of cereals, rapeseed, maize and vegetables. The hilly countryside is no longer typical of the south of France. On the way to Toulouse, the canal is still pleasantly far from larger built-up areas. There are villages within walking or cycling distance for basic provisions and with a post office and a telephone so that you can keep in touch with friends and family. All French telephone boxes have been converted to use the *telecarte* which you can buy in stationers and in shops with a tobacco licence – recognisable by the cigar sign outside. The number of the telephone box is displayed inside if you want to be called back. From the UK you use the 0033 prefix for France and leave off the first zero of the telephone box number.

The double Sanglier lock is the last one with the Midi's traditional 30 metre-long chambers. The lock-lengthening programme for the whole canal has long been shelved. Working backwards from Toulouse, the scheme only reached

Port Lauragais is the home of the Canal du Midi museum.

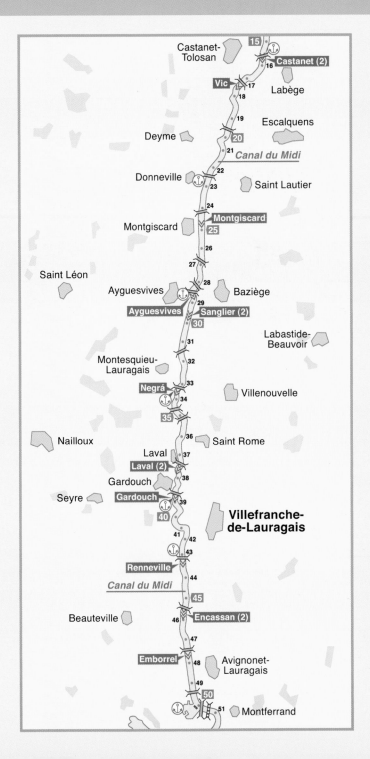

Castanet-Tolosan

15

16 **Castanet (2)**

Labège

Vic **17**

18

19

Escalquens

20

21 *Canal du Midi*

Deyme

22

Donneville

23

Saint Lautier

24

Montgiscard

Montgiscard **25**

26

27

Saint Léon

28

Ayguesvives

29

Baziège

Ayguesvives **Sanglier (2)**

30

31

Labastide-Beauvoir

Montesquieu-Lauragais

32

33

Negra

34

Villenouvelle

35

Nailloux

36

Saint Rome

Laval

37

Laval (2)

38

Gardouch

Seyre

Gardouch

39

40

Villefranche-de-Lauragais

41 **42**

43

Renneville

44

Canal du Midi

45

Beauteville

46 **Encassan (2)**

47

Emborrel

48

Avignonet-Lauragais

49

50

51 Montferrand

You may experience some turbulence in the oval lock at Castanet.

the next lock (Ayguesvives), which was lengthened to 40.5 metres and also converted from a two-chamber lock to a single chamber with a rise/fall of 4.44 metres. Vertical posts set in the lock walls have been conveniently provided to take bow and stern lines.

It is a similar set-up at Montgiscard, the next village; a friendly keeper mans the converted double lock; when we were last there he was doing a great trade in selling fresh eggs. Next to the old wash house is a quay and a water tap. The climb up the path and along the road to the village centre is worth the effort to see the old church with its typical Toulouse bell-tower, from which there is a great view of the hills to the north.

The former double lock at Castanet is the last one on the route to the Atlantic which has the traditional oval-shape chamber. From here on – there are still three Midi locks in the municipal area of Toulouse – the locks have parallel walls, as on most other French waterways. In these newer rectangular chambers less eddies and whirls are created, but unlike the oval locks, two boats cannot always be accommodated one alongside the other because of the uniform width of the chamber.

On this canal section, as in many other parts of France, the towpath has been upgraded to a cycle track, in this case starting at Toulouse. This is no doubt a good idea, although cyclists zipping by can perhaps spoil the isolation of a mooring spot. Those on board seeking peace and quiet can always moor up alongside the opposite bank.

TOULOUSE

In Toulouse, the Canal du Midi loses its identity to some extent as it enters France's fourth largest city. On the outskirts, town planners have tried to maintain the atmosphere of the south. Midiville is the name of a residential district which was designed to create a Mediterranean ambience. Port Sud marina has been constructed 12 kilometres from the city

The expensive apartments of Port Sud on the outskirts of Toulouse.

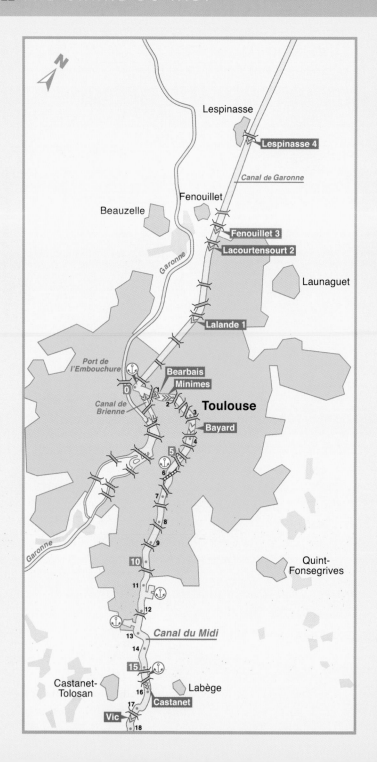

Port St Sauveur in Toulouse has good berths
for visitors.

centre. Here you will find a few canal boats for charter and
yachts with their masts lowered waiting to make the passage
down to the sea. There is usually space to moor alongside the
canal bank, thereby avoiding marina charges at Port Sud and
the curious gazes of residents of the surrounding expensive
waterside apartments.

Between Port Sud and the docks on the north shore, a string
of houseboats have their permanent berths. The French
authorities tolerate this, as long as the boats are kept in good
running order and their owners are prepared to move their
craft if work has to be carried out in this part of the canal.

Toulouse is the centre for France's aeronautical industry. On
one side of the canal is an airfield; on the other are huge
buildings devoted to aviation and space-travel where Airbus
and Ariane were designed and built. Next comes the
University quarter. Here you will find the last peaceful berths
before you approach the city centre, with parks on the left
bank. Then comes yet another canal bridge but this time it

carries the waterway over a four-lane motorway. The sturdy metal trough containing the canal has been colourfully painted on its underside. Two kilometres beyond the decorated pont-canal is the old harbour of Port St Sauveur which, in recent years, has undergone something of a facelift and now provides all the usual facilities for visiting yachts and there is reasonable security.

Beyond the port, the canal is flanked by busy highways until the last kilometre which is again lined with the familiar Midi plane trees. In this final approach to the city centre, there are just three more locks. In order to open the first of these (Bayard) which is right next to the main railway station, you have to pull on rubber poles which are suspended above the water in the approaches. Bayard is a former two-chamber lock which has been converted to a single chamber with a considerable drop of 6.2 metres. There are four floating bollards which rise or fall with the water level, but only one of these may be within easy reach. The lock, however, has been converted so that the water does not gush through the sluices in front of the boat, but is piped into the chamber from underneath, creating only a few eddies.

The next lock, Minimes, has also been converted from a double to a single chamber, but the drop is only just over 4 metres. This lock and the last of the Canal du Midi locks (Bearnais) are operated by a single lock keeper, because the traffic to and from the Canal de Garonne is nowadays pretty thin. A sign requests you to wait, if the keeper is busy at the other lock. But the sign does not say how long you will have to wait.

The Canal du Midi ends at Port l'Embouchure, where a magnificent marble bas-relief decorates the brick-built arches spanning the entrances to three waterways – looking east from the harbour, the Canal de Garonne is to port, in the middle is the Canal du Midi, and to starboard the Canal de Brienne. This hub of inland waterways is encircled by hectic highways. Leaving the port's quayside to visit the centre of the city involves a risky dash across roads, dodging the busy traffic. During the day, the traffic noise is considerable, and the port would not make a peaceful mooring for the night. After the Midi passage through the tranquil countryside, the noisy activity in the centre of Toulouse may come as something of a shock.

The first of the two locks on the Canal de Brienne which connects the end of the Midi to the River Garonne, normally stands open and a slight current feeds this short 1.6-kilometre waterway. At the other end of the Brienne is a functioning but seldom-used lock into the Garonne River. A nearby weir stops Garonne river navigation westwards, but boat trips occasionally lock out from the Brienne on to the Garonne River, giving passengers a fine view of the city. Pleasure boats are not permitted to use this lock or the Garonne river in Toulouse.

Bayard lock, Toulouse has a rise and fall of 6.2 metres.

Those who wish to explore the city at a leisurely pace may decide to look for accommodation ashore. At the back of the Capitole, Toulouse's impressive 18th century town hall, you will find an old tower which houses the tourist office. From the beginning of June until the end of September this is open from Monday to Saturday: 9.00 until 19.00; Sundays and national holidays: 10.30 until 17.15. The rest of the year it is open from Monday to Friday: 9.00 until 18.00: Saturday: 9.00 to 12.30 and 14.00 to 18.00: Sundays and national holidays: 10.00 to 12.30 and 14.00 to 17.00.

Toulouse has, for centuries, attracted considerable wealth and trade. At the time of the construction of the Canal du Midi, the city was the centre for the international trade in dyes evidenced today by the grand houses once occupied by the city's wealthy merchants. There are many historic buildings, notably the world-famous Basilique St-Sernin. It is called the 'red-brick city' because so many of the great buildings were constructed using a pinkish-red building material from the Garonne plain. It has a prestigious ancient university, but most people associate Toulouse with the aerospace industry. Tours are possible of the Aérospatiale Matra-Airbus in Colomiers on the west side of Toulouse and of Cité de l'Espace off the A61 ringroad.

RIVER HÉRAULT

Some of the River Hérault is navigable, although most boats will only experience the 1 kilometre of river which forms part of the Canal du Midi navigation between Agde's flood lock (Prades) and the *Bassin Rond*. The southern maritime end of l' Hérault, accessible through Agde's *Bassin Rond* or from the sea at le Grau-d'Agde, is only available to privately-owned craft. Non-seagoing hire-boats will not be allowed onto the lower part of the river through the third pair of gates in the *Bassin Rond* as the hire companies' boats are not licensed to use the 4.5 kilometres of the maritime Hérault.

The upper section of l'Hérault River can be accessed from the Midi on the Agde side of Prades flood lock (*écluse de garde*) which is normally open. The countryside on this stretch of river is really beautiful. Apart from a couple of anglers' rowing boats, nobody comes this way. The tranquil surroundings are a great haven for wildlife. Kingfishers and rare kinds of heron nest here.

The broad waters of the River Hérault.

The deep water is in the middle of the river (some 2 metres or more). On the banks, when we passed through, trees had toppled into the water and nobody had removed them. After 5 kilometres, the navigable section ends just before the road bridge at Quai Marius, the old harbour at Bessan. But the once busy trade of wine casks from the cellars of the nearby village has long since ceased. The steep bank has been reinforced with boulders, and there is a slipway for smaller boats. Beyond the road bridge, the river narrows and turning would be difficult. Two bends farther on, a weir puts an end to navigation for even the smallest craft.

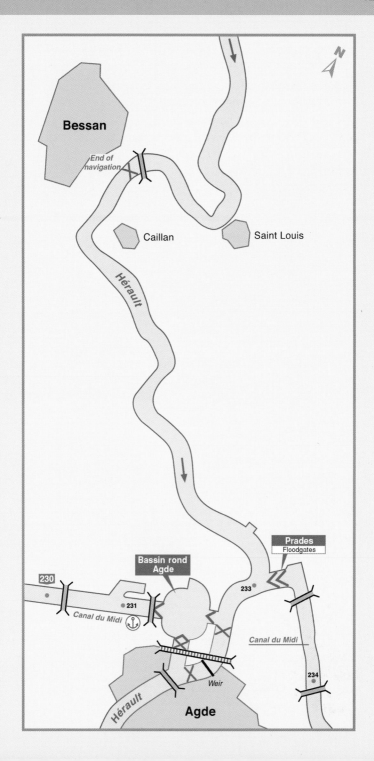

Bessan

End of navigation

Caillan

Saint Louis

Hérault

Prades
Floodgates

Bassin rond
Agde

230

233

231

Canal du Midi

Canal du Midi

234

Weir

Hérault

Agde

CANAL DE LA ROBINE

The Canal de la Robine almost became the southernmost end of the Canal du Midi. During planning in the 17th century, Port-la-Nouvelle and La Franqui, about 10 kilometres to the south, were both possible choices as the Midi's seaport. However, the canal's brilliant architect, Riquet, came up with the idea of building a completely new harbour on the Cap du Sète to handle trans-shipments between inland craft and sea-going vessels. Riquet may have been influenced by the likely silting up of Port-la-Nouvelle and La Franqui or wanted to see his hometown of Béziers linked by the canal to the sea.

A century later, the Canal de la Robine connecting the Canal du Midi with Narbonne and Port-la-Nouvelle was built, largely following a connecting route between the Aude and the Mediterranean which the Romans had constructed. The northernmost 5 kilometres, known as the Canal de Jonction (connecting canal), are newer, although this section is over 200

Entry from the Canal du Midi into the Canal de Jonction.

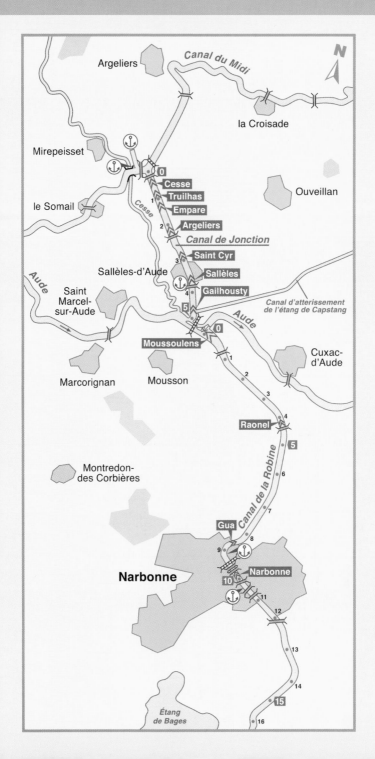

Argeliers

Canal du Midi

la Croisade

Ouveillan

Mirepeisset

le Somail

Cesse

0

Cesse
Truilhas
Empare

1

2

Argeliers

Canal de Jonction

3

Saint Cyr

Sallèles-d'Aude

Sallèles

4

Gailhousty

5

*Canal d'atterissement
de l'étang de Capstang*

Saint
Marcel-
sur-Aude

Aude

0

Aude

Moussoulens

1

Cuxac-
d'Aude

Marcorignan

Mousson

2

3

Raonel

4

5

6

Montredon-
des Corbières

7

Canal de la Robine

Gua

8

9

Narbonne

Narbonne

10

11

12

13

14

15

*Étang
de Bages*

16

years old. The Canal de Jonction and Canal de la Robine are known jointly as the *'Embranchement de la Nouvelle'*.

After the branch-off from the Canal du Midi near Port-la-Robine, the route is dead straight down to the valley of the Aude. The five locks before the town of Sallèles d'Aude are all less than 1 kilometre apart and in sight of each other. The oval-chambered locks have been converted to automatic operation. As soon as the lines are secured, a crew member lands to operate the lock by pressing a button on a box situated half-way along the chamber. Near the Écluse d'Empare (the third from the top) is the Amphoralis (Museum of Amphorae) which has been built right on the spot where Gallo-Roman pottery was discovered. To reach the museum from the lock, you have to cross the tracks of a railway line that, nowadays, is only used by trains carrying sightseers at weekends. A platform has been built here specially for these daytrippers from Narbonne. The museum is open daily from 1 July until 30 September: opening less frequently outside the season. The opening hours are posted at the gate.

Ahead, the first of the locks on the Canal de Jonction.

SALLÈLES D'AUDE

The canal is lined with magnificent umbrella pines and a few cypress trees; on one side is the road to Sallèles; on the other is the railway line for the tourists from Narbonne, making excursions from the town to the Minervois wine-growing region. Shady plane trees now line the canal at Sallèles-d'Aude, the next village, where the canal was been widened to form a turning basin for the *péniches*, and now serves as an attractive, shady *port de plaisance*. The basin was built in the 1980s when plans to upgrade the Canal du Midi also included the Canal de Jonction and Canal de la Robine, lengthening the locks to accommodate 40-metre *péniches*. The last barges transporting wine from here towards Bordeaux disappeared at the beginning of the 1990s when the Canal du Midi had to be closed in the summer for lack of water. Today the *péniches* could travel through the modernised locks from the Rhône to the harbour at Port-la-Nouvelle, but the only commercial shipping using the *'Embranchement de la Nouvelle'* these days are the hotel boats and the *vedettes* loaded with sightseers.

Downstream of Argeliers lock on the
Canal de Jonction.

In the centre of Sallèles, although lots of houses are now unoccupied and some for sale, not all the window shutters are permanently closed as some serve as holiday homes for people from the cities. Those who find washing clothes on board tedious can leave their laundry at Sallèles on the way to the sea and pick it up again two days later on the return journey back to the Midi. The *blanchisserie* at Sallèles is hidden away in a side street and difficult to find without asking.

In the pound above the lock at Sallèles, you can moor up alongside quays which have been refurbished for pleasure boats, but it is very noisy because on both sides of the canal, the road traffic is very hectic. In the lower reaches, the canal surroundings are much more tranquil. The modernisation of the Sallèles lock is a good example of the upgrading carried out. They created a single lock from the existing 2-chamber staircase which explains the 5.4-metre fall/rise. This means that every time Sallèles lock is used, twice as much water

Sallèles lock shaded by plane trees.

flows away downstream as comes from upstream. The water level between locks drops noticeably when several craft go through at short intervals. The canal fills up again, but this can take hours, so when mooring in this section you have to be prepared for varying water levels of 20 or 30 centimetres or more.

At Sallèles lock, which is fitted with vertical mooring posts in the chamber, a stone monument has been erected celebrating the 200th anniversary of this canal, and reminding us of the days when barges were towed by horses. At the next lock (Gailhousty) stands an ornate but nowadays empty building, which at one time was occupied by the inland waterway authority. On the bank here is a display board showing the route along the short section of the River Aude which is well marked with port and starboard navigation marks, and there is a similar board at the other end of the river section for traffic coming the other way.

Gailhousty – the last lock on the Canal de Jonction.

Keep well clear of l'Aude weir (on the right),
just above Moussoulens flood lock.

THE RIVER AUDE

Below Gailhousty lock is a dry dock. The canal, which is narrow here, then widens in a bend to the right into the River Aude which, in a short 700-metre section, links the Canal de Jonction with the Canal de la Robine. Initially you are moving against the Aude's current until you pass beneath some electricity cables, then you must make a wide curve across the river, now with the current, over to its right bank, underneath a railway bridge and through a flood lock (Moussoulens) whose gates are permanently open except when the Aude is in spate. Keep well clear of the weir across the Aude to port, just before the Moussoulens flood lock.

NARBONNE

There are two more locks before reaching the outskirts of Narbonne, where the canal is lined with plane trees and becomes noticeably narrower. The quays in Narbonne have been renovated at great expense. In a sweeping left-hand

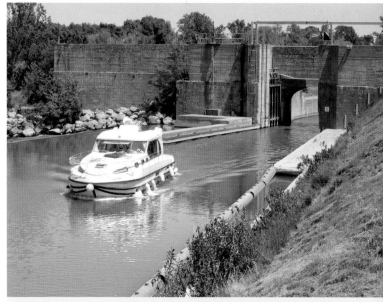

Moussoulens flood lock on the Canal
de la Robine.

bend, the boats at a hire-boat base are moored, on occasions
so densely that they obscure the visibility round the corner.
Next comes Narbonne lock which is situated right in the
middle of the town.

It is automated and fitted with light signals displayed in the
approaches. The locking procedure is started when a rubber
pole which is hanging under a bridge is grasped and turned
through 45° as you motor slowly past. At the lock one of
the crew must disembark to close the gates or open them
again by pressing a button. Previously this lock was a real
challenge for all lighter glassfibre boats as on entering or
leaving, they could be pinned against the opposite bank by
the force of water from a weir. Barriers prevented serious
damage, but it was rare to get past the weir without a bump,
to the delight of the many spectators. This hazard for
pleasure boats has now been eliminated by altering the weir
so that the current from the spillway now runs largely in
the same direction as the canal. Only after heavy rainfall,

The boat may be forced sideways outside Narbonne lock.

when the volume of water is greater, boaters might have difficulties.

Shortly after the lock, the canal passes under the Roman bridge crowded with houses. The arch of the bridge from a distance looks very low. In the centre, however, there is plenty of headroom. With 3 metres' clearance, larger craft like the *vedettes* can tour the waterway with their sightseers. Under the next bridge, the rubber pole is hanging to open Narbonne lock from the opposite direction. After that you are in the centre of the town. The lovely cathedral and the old quarter of the town are only a short walk away.

Opposite you can see the market hall – a spectacular 19th century structure of steel and glass. Right next door to this building is l'Estagnol restaurant, which gave us a good lunch at a reasonable price. It is a pleasure to see that in Narbonne they have thought about pedestrians. Some of the narrow streets are completely closed to motor traffic. The town quays are well supplied with bollards to encourage the crews

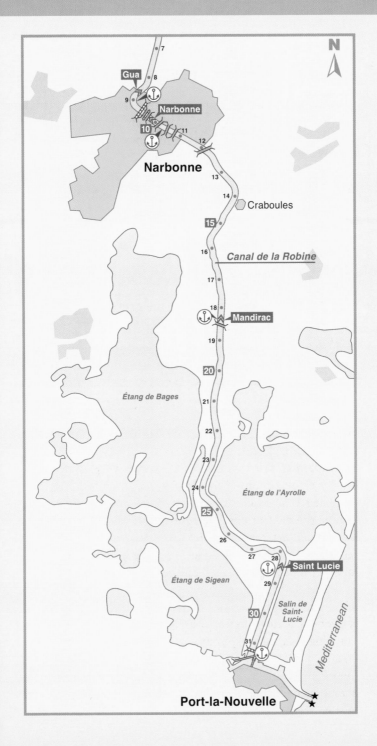

Gua

Narbonne

Narbonne

Craboules

Canal de la Robine

Mandirac

Étang de Bages

Étang de l'Ayrolle

Étang de Sigean

Saint Lucie

Salin de Saint-Lucie

Mediterranean

Port-la-Nouvelle

of pleasure boats to moor up here. However, spending the night alongside Narbonne's quays is only recommended for the noise-tolerant, because there is no escaping the sound, on both sides of the canal, from the traffic of this bustling town.

Narbonne was founded by the Romans in the year 118BC. Today it is difficult to imagine the town as an important port in Roman times. The silting, which causes so much trouble to other towns on the French Mediterranean coast, keeping dredgers constantly in operation in existing harbours, has moved Narbonne 20 kilometres inland, accessible from the sea only by the Canal de la Robine.

For some two and a half kilometres after leaving the town, tall trees along the banks provide some welcome shade, before they dwindle in numbers farther on. Then the only shelter from the sun's rays is beneath the boat's bimini or a large umbrella. On the outskirts of the town, the A9 motorway crosses the canal, and a little farther on, the railway line to Spain runs alongside within 50 metres of the water.

Soon after Mandirac lock (which is worked by a switch) railway track and canal run along a narrow strip of land separating the broad expanses of water of the Bages and Ayrolle *étangs*. The canal, which in sections seems more like a meandering meadow stream, broadens out after a bend to the left. A low, wooded range of hills comes into view, crowned with rocky outcrops, whilst on the bank, you can see reed beds and fig trees. This whole area is a nature reserve, as explained on a sign at Ste Lucie lock. This makes a peaceful berth for the night, barely disturbed by a herd of goats grazing on the narrow tongue of land between the canal and the *étangs*. Cyclists following the canal, which is the most direct route from Narbonne to the sea, are rarely out after nightfall.

Ste Lucie lock, which is the last on the waterway, has two chambers and straight walls. The upper chamber at present is not in operation, but could be used by larger craft by turning the crank handle. The lower chamber is worked by pushing a button. A crew member has to land to operate the control box on the east side of the lock chamber. The drop is less than one metre, the slight variations depending on the sea level at Port-la-Nouvelle. After the lock there is a straight stretch of two and a half kilometres. The water now becomes brackish as the waterway passes between the salt flats and into the harbour of Port-la-Nouvelle and from there into the Mediterranean. For inland water craft, the journey finishes at the end of the straight.

PORT-LA-NOUVELLE

You can tell, as you enter the inland harbour at the end of the canal, that in a seaport such as Port-la-Nouvelle, priority is given to the maritime moorings. Modest berths for visiting canal boats are to be found between a railway and a road bridge on the left-hand side. Entry into the maritime harbour, with its fishing vessels and big ships alongside the quays, is prohibited for inland craft. But sightseeing from the

Ste Lucie – the last lock before the sea.

The inland harbour at Port-la-Nouvelle.

quayside is impressive enough, giving you a close-up view of the large ships that are berthed here.

Those keen to see the sea and sample the beach have a walk of about 2 kilometres from the canal moorings. The built-up area *en route* is mostly holiday accommodation, the nearer you get to the beach. They do not spoil the skyline as the building height is restricted. The broad sandy beach seems to stretch on to infinity.

INDEX